GANDHI, AMBEDKAR, SAVARKAR
HINDU, HINDUISM AND HINDUTVA

About the Author

Prof. Prem Anand Mishra teaches at Faculty of Gandhian Studies, Gujarat Vidyapith, Ahmedabad. He is the author of *Hind Swaraj: A Deconstructive Reading* (2012), *Peace Research: Issues and Application* (2015), *Gandhian Humanism in the Twenty first Century* (2015), *Position: Gandhi's Intervention in Contemporary Discourse* (2017), and Co-author of *Debating Nationalism* (2018). He has also contributed to the renowned *Journal Gandhi Marg*, *Journal of Gandhian Studies* and *The Indian Journal of Political Science*.

GANDHI, AMBEDKAR, SAVARKAR HINDU, HINDUISM AND HINDUTVA

Prem Anand Mishra

CONCEPT PUBLISHING COMPANY PVT. LTD.
NEW DELHI - 110 059

ISBN: 978-93-5594-539-6

First Published 2022

Published and Printed by

Since 1974

Concept Publishing Company Pvt. Ltd.
A/15-16, Commercial Block, Mohan Garden
New Delhi-110059 (India)
T : +91-11-41101460
E: publishing@conceptpub.com, W: www.conceptpub.com

Cataloging in Publication—Courtesy: D.K. Agencies (P) Ltd. <docinfo@dkagencies.com>

Mishra, Prem Anand, author.
Gandhi, Ambedkar, Savarkar : Hindu, Hinduism and Hindutva / Prem Anand Mishra.
pages cm
Includes bibliographical references and index.
ISBN 9789355945396

1. Gandhi, Mahatma, 1869-1948--Political and social views. 2. Ambedkar, B. R. (Bhimrao Ramji), 1891-1956--Political and social views. 3. Savarkar, Vinayak Damodar, 1883-1966--Political and social views. 4. Hinduism--India. 5. Hindutva. 6. Nationalism--India--History--20th century. I. Title.

LCC DS481.G3M57 2022 | DDC 954.035 23

To

…......unknown face of love and hate...

Introduction

In the political and social discourses of India, there is currently a debate of Hinduism and Hindutva. This debate begins with the Indian freedom struggle which was more than overthrowing British colonial power. It was a time of looking back as well. Looking back meant examining our own religion and culture in order to come up with a new vision for India. Looking back challenged several deep-rooted principles, beliefs, and practice prevalent in India's social and cultural life. The intellectuals – leaders and activists of that time re-assessed and re-framed the history, culture, and religion of India. One of the significant aspects of such assessment and reframing was to examine the major religion of India – Hinduism.

The book examines the ways in which Gandhi, Ambedkar, and Savarkar viewed and interpreted Hinduism. Based on their autobiographical accounts and biographical narratives, first, it traces the origin and development of their ideas about Hinduism. Second, reading through the original writings of these three geniuses, it attempts to reconstruct their interpretations of Hinduism. It argues that these three geniuses offer three different worldviews on Hinduism that are non-negotiable.

Gandhi saw Hinduism through an Advaita perspective while Ambedkar saw it through a pragmatic perspective. Hinduism, for Gandhi, represents the highest expression of *ahimsa*, and whatever problems it may face today can be reformed within Hinduism itself. Ambedkar on the other hand rejected Hinduism completely, not only because it has a history of discriminating practice, but because the fundamental philosophical structure of Hinduism is based on inequality. With a distinct perspective, Savarkar attempted to give Hinduism a political meaning. Noting that Hindus need to organize themselves, he developed the concept of Hindutva to accomplish this goal. These three prominent thinkers-activists offer three different modes of interpretation of Hinduism – moral, social, and political.

This book is divided into seven chapters.

Chapter 1 deals with "The Origin and Development of Gandhi's Hinduism". Focusing on Gandhi's Autobiography, it describes how Gandhi in his childhood was influenced by Hindu texts and practices. It also describes how his interest in religious texts developed during his London days (1888-1891), and how he developed it further when he was in South Africa (1893-1915). This chapter presents his journey from an ordinary Hindu child to a modern interpreter and defender of Hinduism through careful selections of his own observations about Hinduism.

Chapter 2 titled "Hinduism and Humiliation: Ambedkar's *Waiting for a Visa*" narrates the origin and development of Ambedkar's critique of Hinduism. It is primarily based on Ambedkar's text *Waiting for a Visa* (1935). Taking nourishment from his biography and other relevant sources, it also explains some of his autobiographical narratives subtexts. It also discusses his disappointment and struggle against the untouchability of Hinduism that eventually led him to declare that although he was born a Hindu, he would not die as a Hindu.

Chapter 3 is titled "The Genesis and Evolution of Savarkar's Hindutva". Savarkar did not write any autobiography, thus, the chapter focus on his three biographies – *Life of Barristeres Savarakar* (1926) by Chitragupta, *Savarkar and his Times* (1950) by Dhananjay Keer, and recently published *Savarkar Echoes from a Forgotten Past* – Part 1 (2019) by Vikram Sampath to trace the origin and development of his notion of Hindutva. The chapter also draws on other recent and relevant studies in order to complement the details in the endevour to trace the origin, and development of his idea of Hindutva.

Chapter 4 "Gandhi and *The Essence of Hinduism*" traces out how Gandhi saw Hinduism and its basic philosophy. Gandhi did not produce a systematic book on Hinduism like Savarkar and Ambedkar but his scattered views on Hindu religion have been compiled and edited by V. B. Kher under the title *The Essence of Hinduism* (1996). This compiled book has been used in this chapter to analyze Gandhi's Hinduism. The chapter focuses on Gandhi's definition of Hindu, Hinduism and its chief characteristics, the division which Gandhi makes between historical Hinduism and philosophical Hinduism, problems within Hinduism and his response to them, and the philosophical structure of Gandhi's Hinduism.

Chapter 5 "Ambedkar's *Philosophy of Hinduism*" focuses on his text 'Philosophy of Hinduism'. The central concern of this chapter is to explore the foundation of Ambedkar's critique of Hinduism that finally, led him to reject it, claiming that inequality is the soul of Hinduism. Besides, the chapter also briefly examines his other writings on Hinduism – *The Hindu Social Order: Its Essential Principles*, *The Hindu Social Order: Its Unique Features*, *Riddles in Hinduism*, and *Annihilation of Caste* to get a comprehensive picture of his critique of Hinduism.

Chapter 6 "Savarkar's *The Essentials of Hindutva*" emphasizes on his text *Hindutva* (1923). Savarkar's Hindutva has taken the place of the Classics in Hindu nationalists' and Hindutva's literature. For those who believe in Hindu Rashtra, it still continues to serve as a major philosophical base. This chapter attempts to show how he defines and constructs the idea of Hindu, Hinduism, and Hindutva. It also examines the arguments of Savarkar focusing on his *Hindu Rashtra Darshan* which is the compilation of his six presidential speeches given to the Hindu Mahasabha from 1937 to 1942.

Chapter 7 "Three Worldviews on Hinduism" attempts to conclude the argument advanced in the book.

The book has certain limitations. It does not discuss the nationalist framework that led these thinkers to reflect on Hinduism and reassess it. Second, it does not compare the thoughts of these prominent thinkers on Hinduism nor does it describe their relations, debates and dialogues related to it. This book has specific reasons for being presented to readers despite these limitations. Today, we observe a kind of appropriation of ideologies to suit political necessities. The danger of this is that it nullifies the radicalism for which the ideologies are known or why they are even relevant today. Political appropriation of an ideology is also a grave injustice to those who have fought and still fight for some social cause taking a particular line of thought and methods. It is in this backdrop that the study wishes to indicate that Gandhi, Ambedkar, and Savarkar offer three different worldviews of Hinduism which are non-negotiable. They define Hinduism in entirely different ways and tones. Unless we have a complete worldview of their ideologies, it is very difficult to discard any appropriation of them made through selective quotations, de-contextualizing them, and presenting them in a quite different manner. This book is a humble attempt to offer worldviews of these three versions of Hinduism. One may note at the end how these three worldviews are unique and uncompromising.

Thanks to all those friends who helped me in conceptualizing the idea for this book. I feel also obligated to those who criticized the theme of this book for digging into the past rather than exploring the crisis of the present. I also feel a kind of gratitude to those well-wishers who tried hard to make me understand how congruence can be achieved by bringing three great thinkers to one platform or to seeing commonality among them. Although I entirely disagree with them, yet this book, in a sense, responds to them.

24 December, 2021 **Prem Anand Mishra**

Contents

1
The Origin and Development of Gandhi's Hinduism

> *The child never learns in afterlife what it does in its first five years ... after birth the child imitates the parents and for a considerable number of years entirely depends on them for this growth* (CWMG 87: 522).[1]

This psychological insight of Gandhi, which he made in his latter part of life, can be applied to trace out the origin and development of his views on Hinduism also. His Autobiography *The Story of My Experiments with Truth,* adequately informs us about his childhood experience in the matter of religion. It also informs us, although heuristically, how his idea of Hinduism gradually developed and took a formal shape in the due course of time. Therefore, reading his autobiography to trace the origin and evolution of his concept of Hinduism is more sensible than looking at other sources.

His Autobiography begins with his family background and his childhood experiences. He notes in his Autobiography that his father was 'truthful, brave and generous, but short-tempered' (Gandhi, 2015:4). He also records that his father had very little 'religious training', but he was exposed to the kind of religious culture that Hindus can gain from frequent visits to temples and listening to religious discourses.He mentions that in his last days, his father began reading the *Gita* at the suggestion of a learned Brahmana friend of the family, and he used to repeat aloud some verses everyday at the time of worship. However, for Gandhi, it was his mother who made an 'outstanding impression' on him by her 'saintliness'. He observes in his Autobiography that his mother was 'deeply religious'. 'She would not think of taking her meals without her daily prayers.'

Gandhi provides a comprehensive details on how her mother was religious. He notes, her mother used to go to *Haveli* – the Vaishnava temple – as her 'daily duties'. She also used to do the *Chaturmas* and she never missed it and she would take the hardest vows and keep them without flinching. Moreover, 'Illness was no excuse for relaxing such vows'. He recalls her once falling ill when she was observing the *Chandrayana* vow, but the illness was not allowed to interrupt the observance. Moreover, 'To keep two or three consecutive fasts was nothing to her'. Not only this, "Living on one meal a day during *Chaturmas* was a habit with her. Not content with that she fasted every alternate day during one *Chaturmas*. During another *Chaturmas* she vowed not to have food without seeing the sun"(*ibid.*, 5). These details might be read in the context of Gandhi's emphasis on vows or *Vrata* developed much later.

In his childhood, Gandhi also read a play *Shravana Pitribhakti,* a play about Shravana's devotion to his parents, with intense interest. After some time he saw an image of Shravana carrying his blind parents on a pilgrimage. Gandhi observes that the book and the picture left 'an indelible impression' on his mind. He also realized that it was an example for him to copy. His heart was captured by another play, Harishchandra. 'Why should not all be truthful like Harishchandra?' It was the question he asked himself day and night. Truth and the ordeals Harishchandra suffered through were the ideals that inspired him. He explains, "I literally believed in the story of Harishchandra. The thought of it all often made me weep. My commonsense tells me today that Harishchandra could not have been a historical character. Still, both Harishchandra and Shravana are living realities" (*ibid.*, 7).

Gandhi learned to know about religion in part rather than through formal education in religion. He writes, "From my sixth or seventh year up to my sixteenth I was at school, being taught all sorts of things except religion. I may say that I failed to get from the teachers what they could have given me without any effort on their part. And yet I kept on picking up things here and there from my surroundings" (*ibid.*, 30). Gandhi viewed religion in its most broad sense, meaning the realization of self or the knowledge of self, not organized religion. Although he was born in the Vaishnava faith, and he frequently visited the *Haveli,* it never appealed to him. He writes, "I did not like its glitter and pomp. Also, I heard rumours of immorality being practiced there and lost all interest in it. Hence, I could gain nothing from the *Haveli"* (*ibid.*, p. 30). But he notes that what he failed to get there he obtained from his nurse, an old servant of the family;

whose affection for him was abundant. He mentions that he was afraid of ghosts and spirits and Rambha, the nurse, suggested, as a remedy for this fear and it was the repetition of Ramanama. He recalls in his Autobiography, "... I began repeating Ramanama to cure my fear of ghosts and spirits. This was, of course, short-lived, but the good seed sown in childhood was not sown in vain. I think it is due to the seed sown by that good woman Rambha that today Ramanama is an infallible remedy for me" (*ibid.*, 30). Also, he mentions that the reading of the *Ramayana* before his sick father made a profound impression on him. During the illness at Porbandar, his father every evening used to listen to the Ramayana. The reader of *Ramayana* was a great devotee of Rama and had a melodious voice. Gandhi was only thirteen years old when it happened and he reminds that this incident laid the foundation of his deep devotion to the *Ramayana*. As he notes in his autobiography, "I regard the *Ramayana* of Tulsidas as the greatest book in all devotional literature" (*ibid.*, 31). Later on, in Rajkot, he attended the reading of another Hindu text the *Bhagavat*, but he found the reciter 'uninspiring'. Much later, he read the Gujarati Version of the *Bhagavat* and heard portions of the original by Pandit Madan Mohan Malaviya during his twenty-one days' fast and found that 'the *Bhagavat* is a book which can evoke religious fervour' (*ibid.*, 31). Gandhi observes in his Autobiography, "Impressions formed at that age strike roots deep down into one's nature, and it is my perpetual regret that I was not fortunate enough to hear more good books of this kind read during that period" (*ibid.*, 31).

In Rajkot, however, he was exposed to various branches of Hinduism and sister religions. His father and mother would visit the *Haveli* besides Shiva's and Rama's temples and would take or send the youngsters there. Jain monks also paid frequent visits to his father, and would even go out of their way to accept food from him. They also talked with his father about religious subjects. Besides, Mussalman and Parsi friends often would talk to his father about their faiths, and his father listened to them with respect, and often with interest. Being his father's nurse, Gandhi often had a chance to be present at these talks. He notes, "These many things combined to inculcate in me toleration for all faiths" (*ibid.*, 32). However, Christianity was at the time an exception. The reason was the Christian missionaries and their conversion policy. Moreover, the new convert, as Gandhi notes, 'abused the religion of his ancestors, their customs and their country'. All these things created in Gandhi a dislike for Christianity. But one thing that took deep root in him was the conviction that "morality is the basis of things, and that truth is the substance of all morality" (*ibid.*, 33). Thus, he notes, "Truth became my sole objective. It began to grow in magnitude everyday and my definition of it also has been ever-widening" (*ibid.*, 33). Further, a Gujarati didactic stanza also gripped his mind and heart. Its precept—return good for evil—became his guiding principle. He notes that "It became such a passion with me that I began numerous experiments in it" (*ibid.*, 33).

Gandhi's views on Hinduism developed considerably in England (1888-1891). Towards the end of his second year in London, he came across two Theosophists, brothers who talked to him about the *Gita*. They were reading Sir Edwin Arnold's translation – *The Song Celestial*-and they invited Gandhi to read the original with them. He writes in his Autobiography, "I felt ashamed, as I had read the divine poem neither in Sanskrit nor in Gujarati. I was constrained to tell them that I had not read the *Gita*, but that I would gladly read it with them, and that though my knowledge of Sanskrit was meagre, still I hoped to be able to understand the original to the extent of telling where the translation failed to bring out the meaning. I began reading the *Gita* with them" (*ibid.*, 64). The verses in the second chapter made a deep impression on his mind. He considered the book as 'one of priceless worth' and 'the *par excellence* for the knowledge of Truth'. In London, he also read *The Light of Asia* by Sir Edwin Arnold, with even greater interest than the reading of the *Bhagavadgita*. He notes, "Once I had begun it I could not leave off'. He also read Madame Blavatsky's *Key to Theosophy* and this book stimulated in him 'the desire to read more books on Hinduism" (*ibid.*, 65). It also disabused him of the notion fostered by the missionaries that Hinduism was rife with superstition. He also studied the *New Testament*, which made a different impression on him, especially the Sermon on the Mount which went straight to his heart. He also compared it with the *Gita*. He stated, "The verses, 'But I say unto you, That ye resist not evil; but whosoever shall smite thee on thy right cheek, turn to him the other also. And if any man takes away thy coat let him have thy cloak too,' delighted me beyond measure and put me in mind of Shamal Bhatt's 'For a bowl of water, give a goodly meal' etc. My young mind tried to unify the teaching of the *Gita*, the *Light of Asia* and the Sermon on the Mount. That renunciation was the highest form of religion appealed to me greatly" (*ibid.*, 66). This reading whetted his appetite for studying the lives of other religious teachers. A friend recommended Carlyle's *Heroes and Hero-Worship* and he read the chapter on the Hero as a prophet and learned of the Prophet's (Mahammad) greatness and bravery and austere living. He mentions that beyond these readings he could not read more on religion but he 'took a mental note of the fact that I should read more religious books, and acquaint myself with all the principal religions' (*ibid.*, 66).

Ironically, in shaping the idea of Hinduism, a Jain Raichandbhai played a significant role in Gandhi's life. Although Gandhi did not enthrone Raichandbhai in his heart as his Guru, Raichandbhai's impact was profound on him, especially his 'state of equipoise'. He writes, "Though I was then groping and could not be said to have any serious interest in religious discussion, still I found his talk of absorbing interest. I have since met many a religious leaders or teachers. I have tried to meet the heads of various faiths, and I must say that no one else has ever made on me the impression that Raychandbhai did. His words went straight home to me. His intellect compelled as great regard from me as his moral earnestness, and deep down in me was the conviction that he would never willingly lead me astray and would always confide to me his innermost thoughts. In my moments of spiritual crisis, therefore, he was my refuge" (*ibid.*, 82).

In terms of religion, Gandhi's years in South Africa were filled with 'religious ferment' and 'comparative study of religions'. It is worth mentioing that it was in South Africa he realized the necessity of diving deeper into the religious studies. As his autobiography informs, his settling down in South Africa was not only about the matter of livelihood and finding an escape from Kathiawad intrigues but, he found himself there 'in search of God and striving for self-realization' (*ibid.*, 147-48). He continued to correspond with Raychandbhai even in South Africa and Raychandbhai guided him in the matter or religion as well.

In South Africa, Gandhi read some Hindu texts in the original form. In 1903,Theosophist friends intended to draw him into their society, with a view to getting something from him as a Hindu. Because Theosophical literature is replete with Hindu influence, these friends expected that Gandhi should be helpful to them. Gandhi explained that his Sanskrit study was not much to speak of. He also admitted before them that he had not read the Hindu scriptures in the original, and that even his acquaintance with the translations was of the slightest. But being believers in *sanskara* (tendencies caused by previous births) and *punarjanma* (rebirth) theosophists assumed that Gandhi should be able to render at least some help. Gandhi notes that he felt like 'a Triton among the minnows' (*ibid.*, 243). Thus he started reading Swami Vivekananda's *Raja yoga* with some of these friends and M.N. Dvivedi's *Rajayoga* with others. He also studied Patanjali's *Yoga Sutras* and the *Bhagavadgita*.

With some friends, he formed a sort of Seekers' Club where they had regular readings. Gandhi had already faith in the *Gita*, which had a kind of fascination for him. He had one or two translations of *Gita*, through which he tried to understand the original Sanskrit. He also decided to get by heart one or two verses of the *Gita* everyday. For this purpose, he employed the time of his morning ablutions. He notes, "The operation took me thirty-five minutes, fifteen minutes for the toothbrush and twenty minutes for the bath. The first I used to do standing in Western fashion. So on the wall opposite I stuck slips of paper on which were written the *Gita* verses and referred to them now and then to help my memory. This time was found sufficient for memorizing the daily portion and recalling the verses already learnt. I remember having thus committed to memory thirteen chapters" (*ibid.*, 244). This reading of the *Gita* convinced Gandhi to claim it as 'an infallible guide of conduct' and the 'dictionary of daily reference' (*ibid.*, 244). He mentions, "Just as I turned to the English dictionary for the meanings of English words that I did not understand, I turned to this dictionary of conduct for a ready solution of all my troubles and trials" (*ibid.*, 244).

In 1905, Gandhi delivered a public discourse on Hinduism. In March 1905, he delivered the first of a series of four lectures on *Hinduism* at the Masonic Temple under the auspices of the Johannesburg Lodge of the Theosophical Society (CWMG 4: 368). He introduced his subject by remarking that the endeavours of the Johannesburg Lodge to promote interest in the study of different religious systems were most praiseworthy. Continuing, the lecturer Gandhi described what was meant by the title 'Hindu', and referred it to "the branch of the Aryan people that had migrated to the trans-Indus districts of India, and had colonised that vast country" (CWMG 4: 368). Aryanism, he felt, would have been a more suitable description of the faith practiced by so many Indians, than Hinduism.

He mentioned that one of the most remarkable characteristics of the religion professed by Hindus was self-abnegation. He observes this can be obviously seen in the name of the religion itself, for, unlike most of the great world religions, it did not "derive its name from any prophet or teacher, although it counted some of the greatest within its fold" (*ibid.*, 368). Gandhi further noted in the lecture that the Hindus themselves claimed that the date of their scriptures was veiled in the midst of antiquity. Moreover, the scriptures themselves are God-given. He also stated that over two hundred millions of people professed Hinduism, and this faith entered into their every act. The key-note of Hinduism on the spiritual side is *moksha* or salvation; that is, the final absorption of the Soul in the Infinite Soul that pervades all things. He noted that concerning religion, pantheism is the chief characteristic of Hinduism, whilst, on the ethical plane, self-abnegation is the most notable quality, with its corollary, toleration. In social matters, the characteristic of caste is predominant, whilst the ceremonial characteristic is the sacrificing of animals.

He further elaborated the Hinduism, "At a time when the faith of the Hindus had become more formal, Prince Gautama Buddha, having learnt the spiritual worth of things during a prolonged period of contemplation, commenced to teach that animal sacrifices were despiritualising, and that the highest form of love was expressed by extending that toleration, which was already a tenet of their faith, in the direction of refraining from killing or otherwise destroying living things" (*ibid.*, 369). He also cited in the lecture that "Hinduism had never, as a religion, been missionary, as were Christianity and Mahomedanism, but, under King Ashoka, the Buddhist priests were sent far and wide to propagate the new belief" (*ibid.*, 369). He also pointed out that Buddhism had a 'reforming effect upon Hinduism' (*ibid.*, 369), somewhat similar to that of Protestantism upon Catholicism. However, he noted that there was a 'great difference' in the spirit underlying that reform. He argues that no Hindu bore the Buddhist any ill-will, that cannot be said about the Protestants and Catholics. In this connection, he briefly referred to Jainism as the most interesting form of faith. The Jains claimed that it was altogether independent of Buddhism, not a growth from it. Unlike others, they did not claim for the faith that it was of Divine origin, recognizing that its sacred writings were the results of human workmanship.

The second lecture was given by him on 11 March, 1905 in the same Hall. It was devoted to what might be termed the 'second epoch of Hinduism' (*ibid.*, 375). In this lecture, he discussed what happened after the reformation that took place from within, under the influence of the teachings of Buddha. He observed that Hinduism was deeply addicted to idolatry. Several explanations were offered in extenuation, but he could not deny the fact that the Hindus seemingly revered stocks and stones. He noted that the Hindu philosophers easily recognized and worshipped God as the purest spirit and Pantheism took them to the highest flight. It similarly brought down the ignorant masses to the lowest depths. He argued that if the infant mind could not realise God as a pure spirit, it had no difficulty in worshipping Him through His various manifestations. "Many worship Him through the sun, the moon, and the stars, and many worship Him through stocks and stones also, a mode of worship to which philosophical Hinduism, with its tolerant spirit, had no difficulty in reconciling itself. So the wheel of Hindu life went merrily on until there arose in the desert of Arabia a power that was destined to revolutionise ideas and to leave a permanent impress" (*ibid*., 376).

The third lecture of the series was given next Saturday at 8 o'clock in the Masonic Temple. The reports of the third and fourth lectures are not available. However, a summary of the four lectures was later published by him in his journal *Indian Opinion* on 15-4-1905 titled 'Lectures on Religion' (CWMG 4: 405).

He writes that 'the manners of the Hindus and other Indians are almost identical'. He also provides the originality of Hindus. He states, 'Hindus are not considered to be the original inhabitants of India' (*ibid*., 405). Referring to the Western scholars, he mentions that the Hindus, as well as most of the European peoples, lived at one time in Central Asia. Later on, migrating from there, some went to Europe, some to Iran, others moved southeastwards down into India through Punjab, and there spread the Aryan religion. He also provides the detail of the Hindu population and mentions that the Hindu population in India exceeds two hundred million. In his words, "They are called Hindus because they once lived beyond the river Sindhu (Indus). The Vedas are their oldest scripture. Very devout Hindus believe that the Vedas are of divine origin and without beginning" (*ibid*., 405). Referring again to the Western scholars, he noted that the Vedas were composed before 2000 B.C. However, 'The famous Mr. Tilak of Poona has shown that the Vedas must be at least 10,000 years old'. He also pointed out how Hindus are different from others. "The main thing that distinguishes the Hindus is their belief that the Brahman or over soul is all-pervading. What we all have to attain is *moksha* or liberation, *moksha*, here meaning freeing oneself from the evil of birth and death and merging in the Brahman" (*ibid*., 406). As far as the ethics of Hinduism is concerned the chief qualities are humility and even-mindedness. He also recognized that caste reigns supreme in Hindu's temporal affairs. He mentions that the Hindu religion underwent its 'first trial' on the advent of Lord Buddha.

Mentioning this 'first trial' he describes that at the time of the Buddha who was born before 600 B.C., the Hindus were under the glamour of the outward form of their religion. The Brahmins had, out of selfishness, abandoned their true function of defending the Hindu faith. Lord Buddha tried to reduce such a plight. He renounced the world and started doing penance. After spending several years in devout contemplation, he ultimately suggested some reforms in the Hindu religion. His reforms 'greatly affected the minds of the Brahmins, and the killing of animals for sacrifice was stopped to a great extent.' Gandhi argues that it cannot be said that the Buddha founded a new or different religion. However, those who came after him gave his teachings the identity of a separate religion. Later on, Gandhi describes, "King Ashoka the Great sent missionaries to different lands for the propagation of Buddhism, and spread that religion in Ceylon, China, Burma and other countries" (*ibid.*, 406). He mentions that one may notice the 'distinctive beauty of Hinduism' revealed in this process and it was; no one was converted to Buddhism by force. "People's minds were sought to be influenced only by discussion and argument and mainly by the very pure conduct of the preachers themselves. It may be said that, in India at any rate, Hinduism and Buddhism were but one, and that even today the fundamental principles of both are identical" (*ibid.*, 406). Moreover, he noted that 'Buddhism had a salutary effect on Hinduism' (*ibid.*, 406).

In his summary, Gandhi also described the birth of Prophet Mahomed. Providing the historical details he noted that a thousand years ago, 'the Hindu religion came under another influence' which was 'more profound' (*ibid.*, 406). Hazrat Mahomed, born 1300 years ago, found moral anarchy rampant in Arabia; Judaism was struggling for survival; Christianity was not able to gain a foothold in the land, and the people were busy in self-indulgence. Finding all these improper, caused Mahomad mental agony; and in the name of God, he determined to make them realise their miserable condition. His feeling was so intense that he was able to impress the people around him with his fervour, and Islam spread very rapidly. Gandhi observes that zeal or passion was then a distinct specialty of Islam. It served as a mighty force. This resulted in many positive deeds and sometimes terrible ones too. Providing the details of Islam in India, he mentions in his summary that a thousand years ago the army of Ghazni invaded India to spread Islam. In this invasion, Hindu idols were broken and it advanced as far as Somnath. Islam, however, had a dual impact. On the one hand, violence was thus being used to spread Islam, on the other, the Muslim saints were unfolding the real merit of Islam. Gandhi also mentions that the Islamic principle of equality and fraternity made 'a favourable impression especially on the lower classes of Hindus and hundreds of thousands of such Hindus accepted the Islamic faith' (*ibid.*, 407). This created a 'great commotion' in the whole community. He mentions the medieval saint Kabir in this part of his summary and points out his philosophy. According to Kabir, Gandhi stated that Hindu philosophy does not make any distinction between a Hindu and a Muslim.

Both of them, if they did good works, would find a place in heaven. Kabir also emphasized that idolatry was not an essential part of Hinduism. He notes that Kabir tried to bring about a synthesis between Hinduism and Islam, but it did not have much effect. Kabir's philosophy became no more than a distinct sect, and it exists even today. Gandhi also mentions medieval saint Guru Nanak who accepted the reasoning of Kabir and made a similar attempt to fuse the two religions. However, in the process, Nanak felt that Hinduism should be defended against Islam, if necessary, with the sword. This resulted in the birth of Sikhism which produced the Sikh warriors. He further observes that the consequence of all this is that despite the prevalence of Hinduism and Islam as the two principal religions of India today, both the communities live together in peace and amity. Not only this, he notes both are considerate enough not to hurt one another's feelings, save for the bitterness caused by political machinations and excitement. He also says that there is very little difference between a 'Hindu *yogi*' and a 'Muslim fakir' (*ibid.*, 407).

After Islam, Gandhi summarizes the impact of Christianity on Hinduism. "While Islam and Hinduism were thus vying with each other, the Christians landed at the port of Goa about 500 years ago, and set about converting Hindus to Christianity" (*ibid.*, 407). He notes that they also partly resorted to force and converted Hindus partly through persuasion. Some tender-hearted and kind Christian saints also made a 'deep impression' on the lower classes of Hindu society. However, he argues that when Christianity and Western civilization came to be associated, the Hindus began to look upon Christianity with disfavour. Thus he notes, "today, we see few Hindus embracing Christianity in spite of the fact that the Christians are ruling over a vast kingdom" (*ibid.*, 407). Nevertheless, Gandhi mentions the considerable influence of Christianity on Hinduism. "Christian priests imparted education of a high order and pointed out some of the glaring defects in Hindus" (*ibid.*, 407). This resulted in the introspection of some of the Hindu teachers who began to teach the Hindus 'what was good in Christianity' and 'appealed to them to remove these defects' (*ibid.*, 407). This included leaders like Raja Ram Mohan Rai, Devendranath Tagore, and Keshab Chandra Sen. Similarly, in Western India, leaders like Dayanand Saraswati arose and the numerous reformist associations like the Brahmo Samaj and the Arya Samaj came into existence. Gandhi claimed that they all developed in India as a result of Christian influence. On the other hand, Madame Blavatsky came to India, warned both Hindus and Muslims of the evils associated with Western civilization. She asked them to avoid becoming enamoured with it.

On the basis of the above analysis, in the subtitle 'Tenets of Hinduism' Gandhi emphasizes that there have been 'three assaults on Hinduism', coming from Buddhism, Islam and then Christianity (*ibid.*, 408). But, on the whole, he argues, it came out of them 'unscathed'. He points out that Hinduism has tried to imbibe 'whatever was good' in each of these religions. Gandhi then underlines the central tenets of Hinduism as follows: "God exists, He is without beginning, immaculate, and without any attribute or form. He is omnipresent and omnipotent. His original form is Brahman. It neither does, nor causes to be done. It does not govern. It is bliss incarnate, and by it all this is sustained. The soul exists, and is distinct from the body. It also is without a beginning, without birth. Between its original form and the Brahman, there is no distinction. But it takes on, from time to time, a body as a result of *karma* or the power of *maya*, and goes on being born again and again into high or low species in accordance with the good or bad deeds performed by it. To be free from the cycle of birth and death and be merged in Brahman is *moksha* or liberation. The way to achieve this *moksha* is to do pure and good deeds; to have compassion for all living beings, and to live in truth. Even after reaching this stage, one does not attain liberation, for one has to enjoy embodied existence as a consequence of one's good deeds as well" (*ibid.*, 408).

Gandhi provides some deeper explanations after describing these tenets of Hinduism. He writes that one should 'go one step further'. One needs to continue to act, without cherishing any attachment to one's actions. That is, action should be undertaken for its own sake, without an eye on the fruit. How can it be done? He notes that 'everything should be dedicated to God'. Moreover, "We should not cherish, even in a dream, the feeling of pride that we do or can do anything. We should look upon all equally" (*ibid.*, 408). He mentions that these are the beliefs or tenets of Hinduism, however, there are a number of schools in Hinduism. Moreover, "there have arisen a few factions or sects resulting from [differences in] secular practices" (*ibid.*, 409).

He concludes the summary of his lectures by pointing out 'an appeal to the audience'. He, in this appeal, equates Hindus with Indians and notes "anyone of you has been favourably impressed and has come to feel that the Hindus or the Indians, in whose country the religion expounded above prevails, cannot be altogether an inferior people, you can render service to my countrymen even without becoming involved in political matters" (*ibid.*, 409). It is imperative to note the term 'by you'. Gandhi is pointing to Englishmen or others rather than Hindus and Muslims of India. Second, he separates religious from political matters.

It is remarkable because he knows that the fusion of religion with politics may create problems. He also provides the basis of all religions noting that 'all religions teach that we should all live together in love and mutual kindness'. Finally, he says that it was not his intention to preach anyone a sermon as he is not fit to do so. However, as he concludes, "if it has produced any favourable impression on your mind, I would appeal to you to let my brethren have its benefit and, as behoves the English people, to defend them, whenever they are maligned" (CWMG 4: 409).

Gandhi's ideas on Hinduism can also be found in one of his significant articles written in response to Lord Curzon's speech given in Calcutta. On 1 April, 1905, Gandhi wrote an article titled 'Oriental Ideal of Truth' (CWMG 4: 392). It had a reference to Lord Curzon's speech made in his Convocation address at Calcutta University. Lord Curzon has proclaimed in his Convocation address that "the highest ideal of truth is to a large extent a Western conception", and that "undoubtedly truth took a high place in the moral codes of the West before it had been similarly honoured in the East, where craftiness and diplomatic wile have always been held in much repute" (*ibid.*, 392). Responding to Curzon's above-proclaimed statement Gandhi cited the oriental scriptures, and other religious and ethical works on Truth to falsify His Excellency's proclamation. He also wrote that 'if Lord Curzon has any regard for Truth and for the people of this country', he must withdraw 'his baseless and offensive imputations' (*ibid.*, 392).

First of all, he quoted *The Sama Veda, Aranya-Gana, Arka-Parva* to describe the Hindu notion of truth and peace: Conquer wrath with peace; untruth with Truth. After that, he cited *Mundaka Upanishad*, III, 1-6 which states, "Truth alone prevails and not untruth. Truth is the pathway which learned men tread. It is by this path that the sages, satiated in their desires, have obtained salvation in Him who is the infinite ocean of Truth" (*ibid.*, 392). He then cited *Taittiriya Upanishad, I-II-I* noting that the very first injunction given to a disciple after he has taken the sacred thread and entered upon his studies is, 'Speak the Truth, observe duty, do not swerve from Truth'. He writes that according to Hinduism, as mentioned in *Taittiriya II-I-I*, 'Truth is the very essence of Brahma: Brahma is Truth eternal, intelligence immeasurable' (*ibid.*, 392). Then he mentions *Mahanarayan Upanishad XXVII.I,* which states, 'Speech rests on Truth; everything rests on Truth. Therefore, they call Truth the highest'. He quotes the Mahabharata which states, "There is no duty higher than Truth and no sin more heinous than untruth. Indeed, Truth is the very foundation of Righteousness" (*ibid.*, 392).

Taking help from Professor Max Muller's translation, Gandhi also narrated an incident in the *Ramayana*. In this incident, prince Rama was exhorted by a courtier priest to disown his father's promise that he should be banished for fourteen years, but the prince replied, "Truth and mercy are immemorial characteristics of a king's conduct. Hence, the royal rule is in its essence truth. On truth the world is based. Both sages and gods have esteemed truth. The man who speaks truth in this world attains the highest imperishable state. Men shrink with fear and horror from a liar as from a serpent. In this world the chief element of virtue is truth. It is called the basis of everything. Truth is lord in the world, virtue always rests on truth. All things are founded on truth; nothing is higher than it. Why should I not be true to my promise, and faithfully observe the truthful injunction given by my father? Neither through covetousness or delusion nor ignorance will I, overpowered by darkness, break through the barrier of truth, but remain true to my promise by my father. How shall I, having promised to him that I would reside in the forest, transgress his injunction and do what Bharata recommends" (*ibid.*, 392).

Gandhi mentions that laws of nature are expressions of Truth, and virtues are but forms of Truth and all vices are forms of untruth. To support his arguments, Gandhi quotes *Shanti Perva* of *Mahabharata* (Mahabharata, Shanti Parva, CLXII, 8, 9) in which Bhishma says as follows, "Truthfulness, equability, self-control, absence of self-display, forgiveness, modesty, endurance, absence of envy, charity, a noble well-wishing towards others, self-possession, compassion, and harmlessness – surely these are the thirteen forms of Truth." Gandhi also notes the metaphysical character of truth, as depicted in Hinduism especially in *Shanti Perva* . He writes that Truth is That which Is, and Untruth is That which Is Not. He quotes Shanti perva (Mahabharata, Shanti Parva, CLXII, 5) again 'Truth is eternal Brahman.... Everything rests on Truth'. He cites the *Ashvamedha Parva* of the *Mahabharata*, in which Shri Krishna has stated, 'Truth and Dharma ever dwell in me'. He further quotes *Ramayana* which says about truth, "There is nothing greater than Truth, and Truth should be esteemed the most sacred of all things" (*ibid.*, 392-93).

According to Hinduism, *Ishvara* himself is Truth. He quotes *Bhagvatpurana*, XII, 26, "O True of promise, True of purpose, triply True, the Fount of Truth, and dwelling in the True, the Truth of Truth, the eye of Right and Truth, Spirit of Truth, refuge we seek in Thee" (*ibid.*, 393). He also quotes *Bhagvat Gita*, XVI, 1-3 in which Shri Krishna mentions about 'fearlessness, Sattvik purity, steadfast pursuit of wisdom, charity, control of the senses, sacrifice, study, austerity, uprightness; Harmlessness, truthfulness, absence of anger, designation, peace of mind, avoidance of calumny, pity for all beings, absence of greed, gentleness, modesty, absence of restlessness; Energy, forgiveness, endurance, purity, freedom from hatred and from pride—these are his who is born to the divine qualities' (*ibid.*, 393).

Gandhi describes the tenfold law as laid down by Manu, which provides the qualities necessary for reaching the highest Truth, the one Reality: endurance, patience, self-control, integrity, purity, restraint of senses, wisdom, learning, truth, and the absence of anger (*Manusmriti*, VI, 92). Further, he mentions, "Elsewhere they are briefly described as follows: Harmlessness, truth, integrity, purity, control of the senses, said Manu, is the summarised law of the four castes" (*Manusmriti,* x, 63) (CWMG 4: 394). Gandhi observes that Aryan sacred books inculcate the constant practice of righteousness and performance of duty as *Manusmirti* mentions, "The man who is unrighteous, or he who gains wealth by falsehood, or he whoever delights in injuring, never obtains happiness in this world. Although suffering from unrighteousness, let him not turn his mind to unrighteousness; he will behold the speedy overthrow of the unrighteous, of the sinners. Unrighteousness, practiced in this world, does not bear fruit at once like a cow; slowly reacting it cuts off the very roots of the doer'(Manusmriti, IV, 170-172) (CWMG 4: 394).

Gandhi cites *Hitopdesh* which notes that those whose eating is solely for sustaining life, and whose speech is only to proclaim truth, overcome difficulties. He also mentions the ethics of Buddhism that describe four sins of speech: (a) Lying, (b) Slander, (c) Abuse, and (d) Unprofitable conversation. Further, he mentions the Sikh Teaching that holds that truth and falsehood stand to one another in relation of a stone to an earthen vessel. If a stone is thrown at an earthen vessel, the latter will break. In either case it is the earthen vessel that suffered. Finally, Gandhi concludes his article by quoting Kabir who said, 'No act of devotion can equal Truth; no crime is so heinous as falsehood; in the heart where Truth abides, there is My abode' (CWMG 4: 394). Here it must be pointed out that his position on Hinduism as depicted above remained the same till his South African days. This reflects from his letter to Jamnadas, dated 30 May, 1913 (CWMG 12: 93). In his Autobiography, we also find details of what Gandhi read about Hinduism in South Africa. In South Africa he read Max Muller's book *India – What Can It Teach Us?*, and the translation of the Upanishads published by the Theosophical Society. He notes that 'All this enhanced my regard for Hinduism, and its beauties began to grow upon me. It did not, however, prejudice me against other religions. I read Washington Irving's *Life of Mahomet and His Successors* and Carlyle's *Panegyric on the Prophet*. These books raised Mahammad in my estimation. I also read a book called *The Sayings of Zarathustra*' (Gandhi, 2015: 148).

The readings of these texts made an impact on Gandhi of a different kind. He notes that he not only gained more knowledge of different religions, but it also stimulated his self-introspection. Moreover, it inspired him to put into practice whatever appealed to him. For instance, he mentions that he began some of the Yogic practices as he could understand them from a reading of the Hindu books. However, he could not get very far, and decided to follow them with the help of some experts when he returned to India.

Most significantly some Hindu philosophical terms like *aparigraha* (non-possession) and *samabhava* (equability) caught his attention. Further, how to cultivate and preserve that equability was the question for him. He notes that English law was useful to him. He writes in his Autobiography, "Snell's discussion of the maxims of equity came to my memory. I understood more clearly in the light of the *Gita* teaching the implication of the word 'trustee'. My regard for jurisprudence increased, I discovered in it religion. I understood the *Gita* teaching of non-possession to mean that those who desired salvation should act like the trustee who, though having control over great possessions, regards not an iota of them as his own. It became clear to me as daylight that non-possession and equability presupposed a change of heart, a change of attitude" (*ibid.*, 244-45). It is significant to note that it is here Gandhi tried to explore the possibility of a combination of polity and religion.

His Autobiography contains an interesting point where he describes how his reading of Hindu religious texts led him to judge Hindu rituals. This is about the *sacred thread* and *kanthi*. During the trip of Hrishikesh and Lakshman Jhula, a Hindu Swami asked him about *the sacred thread* and *Kanthi*. He convinced Gandhi to have them both, but Gandhi replied, "I will not wear the sacred thread, for I see no necessity for it, when countless Hindus can go without it and yet remain Hindu. Moreover, the sacred thread should be a symbol of spiritual regeneration, presupposing a deliberate attempt on the part of the wearer at a higher and purer life. I doubt whether in the present state of Hinduism and of India, Hindus can vindicate the right can come only after Hinduism has purged itself of untouchability, has removed all distinctions of superiority and inferiority, and shed a host of other evils and shams that have become rampant in it. My mind, therefore, rebels against the idea of wearing the sacred thread. But I am sure your suggestion about the *shikha* is worth considering. I once used to have it, and I discarded it from a false sense of shame. And so I feel that I should start growing it again. I shall discuss the matter with my comrades" (*ibid.*, 364). The Swami did not appreciate his position with regard to the sacred thread. Gandhi notes in his autobiography, "Even today my position remains about the same as it was *Hrishikesh*. So long as there are different religions, every one of them may need some outward distinctive symbol. But when the symbol is made into a fetish and an instrument of proving the superiority of one's religion over others, it is fit only to be discarded. The sacred thread does not appear to me today to be a means of uplifting Hinduism. I am therefore indifferent to it" (*ibid.*, 364).

To trace the development of Gandhi's views on Hinduism, we may note one of his articles published on 6 October, 1921 titled 'Hinduism' (for complete text see Annexure 1 ; CWMG 21: 245-50). About this article, he wrote in *Young India* on 29 January, 1925, "Pretty long while ago, I once wrote in *Young India* an article on Hinduism, which I consider to be one of my most thoughtful writings on the subject. The definition of Hinduism which I gave in it is probably the clearest that I have ever given" (Gandhi 1996: 29). Before writing it, earlier on 21 September, 1921, he made a speech in a public meeting at Dindigul in which he said, 'I claim to be a sanatani Hindu with a due sense of my responsibility to my religion" (CWMG 21: 160). In another public meeting at Kanadukathan on 26 September, 1921, he again called himself a *sanatani* Hindu 'who has lived for over forty years as a true Hindu' (CWMG 21: 183). It is pertinent to note that in both these meetings Gandhi called himself 'a *sanatani* Hindu' in reference to discussion on the problem of untouchability in Hinduism.

His article 'Hinduism' is worth considering here in detail. In this article, he clarified his views on 'Sanatani Hindu'. It needs to be mentioned that he begins his article again with a reference to 'dealing with the problem of untouchability' and it is in this context that he asserted his 'claim to being a Sanatani Hindu'. In his words, "...I have asserted my claim to being a Sanatani Hindu with greater emphasis than hitherto, and yet there are things which are commonly done in the name of Hinduism, which I disregard" (CWMG 21: 245). He also wrote that he had no desire to be called a sanatani Hindu or any other if he was not such. He also mentioned that he did not have any desire to steal in a reform or abuse under the cover of the great faith of Hinduism. Thus he found it necessary 'once for all' to give his 'meaning of sanatana Hinduism' (*ibid.*, 245). He emphasized that he used the word 'sanatana' in its natural sense. He gave the reason why he called himself Sanatani Hindu. In his words, 'I call myself a sanatani Hindu, because, 1. I believe in the Vedas, the Upanishads, the Puranas and all that goes by the name of Hindu scriptures, and therefore in *avatars* and rebirth, 2. I believe in the varnashrama dharma in a sense in my opinion strictly Vedic but not in its present popular and crude sense, 3. I believe in the protection of the cow in its much larger sense than the popular, 4. I do not disbelieve in idol-worship' (*ibid.*, 246).

Gandhi makes every point clear in his article. He writes that he intentionally 'refrained' from using the word 'divine origin in reference to the Vedas or any other scriptures' as he did not believe in the exclusive divinity of the Vedas. He mentioned that he believed the Bible, the Koran, and the Zend-Avesta to be as much divinely inspired as the Vedas. Furthermore, he noted that 'My belief in the Hindu scriptures does not require me to accept every word and every verse as divinely inspired' (*ibid.*, 246). He also stated that although he does not have 'any first-hand knowledge' of these wonderful books, however, he could claim 'to know and feel the truths of the essential teaching of the scriptures'. He also declined 'to be bound by any interpretation', however, learned it may be, 'if it is repugnant to reason or moral sense'. He mentioned that he believes "implicitly in the Hindu aphorism, that no one truly knows the Shastras who has not attained perfection in innocence (*ahimsa*), truth (*satya*) and self-control (*brahmacharya*) and who has not renounced all acquisition or possession of wealth." He also noted that although he believed in the 'institution of gurus, in this age, millions must go without a *guru*, because it was a rare thing to find a combination of perfect purity and perfect learning' (*ibid.*, 246). He argues that one need not despair of ever knowing the truth of one's religion, because 'the fundamentals of Hinduism as of every great religion are unchangeable, and easily understood' (*ibid.*, 246). He observes that every Hindu believes in God and his oneness, in rebirth and salvation. He further asserts what distinguishes Hinduism from every other religion and they are, in his view, its cow-protection and varnashrama (*ibid.*, 246).

In Gandhi's opinion, Varnashrama is 'inherent in human nature', and Hinduism has simply 'reduced it to a science'. It does attach to birth and a man cannot change his *varna* by choice. Further, in his view, not to abide by one's *varna* is to disregard the law of heredity. His argument is that its division into numerous castes is an 'unwarranted liberty taken with the doctrine'. The four divisions are 'all-sufficing' and they 'define a man's calling', 'define duties', and they confer 'no privileges'. Further, these divisions do not restrict or regulate social interaction. Thus he holds that it is against the 'genius of Hinduism' to arrogate to oneself a higher status or assign to another a lesser position. Gandhi points out that all are born to serve God's creation. This includes a Brahmin with his knowledge, a Kshatriya with his power of protection, a Vaisya with his commercial ability and a Sudra with his bodily labour.

Yet it does not mean one should confine his duty to oneself to the *verna* in which he was born and undermine other works. The *verna* gives only a hint of what is 'special quality', 'predominant' and most 'fitting' for one. There is no question of superiority and inferiority in it. Thus, if a Brahmin who claims superiority by right of knowledge falls and has no knowledge. And so with the others who pride themselves on their special qualities. Gandhi claims that 'Varnashrama is self-restraint and conservation and economy of energy' (*ibid.*, 247). He also notes the problem of inter-dining and inter-marriage in Hinduism. He argues that varnashrama is not affected by inter-dining or inter-marriage, yet Hinduism does most emphatically discourage inter-dining and inter-marriage between divisions. He mentions that 'self-denial is no test of varna and a Brahmin may remain a Brahmin, though he may dine with his Sudra brother if he has not left off his duty of service by knowledge. Thus, a Hindu who refuses to dine with another out of a sense of superiority misrepresents his *dharma*. He warns that Hinduism is in danger of losing its substance if it becomes merely a matter of elaborate rules as to what and with whom to eat. He agrees that abstemiousness from intoxicating drinks and drugs, and from all kinds of foods, especially meat, is undoubtedly a great aid to the evolution of the spirit, however, it is by no means an end in itself.

For Gandhi, instead of Varnashram, 'the central fact of Hinduism is cow-protection' (*ibid.*, 248). Cow-protection, for him, is 'one of the most wonderful phenomena in human evolution'. He argues that cow-protection takes 'the human being beyond his species'. The cow, for him, means not a particular animal but 'the entire sub-human world'. In his article, he describes the cow in India as 'the best companion', 'the giver of plenty', 'a poem of pity', 'mother to millions of Indian mankind' (*ibid.*, 248). On this basis, he notes that the protection of the cow means protection of the whole dumb creation of God. He observes that cow-protection is 'the gift of Hinduism to the world' and claims that 'Hinduism will live so long as there are Hindus to protect the cow'. He also writes that Hindus will be judged not by their *tilaks*, not by the correct chanting of *mantras*, not by their pilgrimages, not by their most punctilious observance of caste rules but by their ability to protect the cow. In his view, cow-protection should be done by *tapasya*, by self-purification, and by self-sacrifice. In his view, the best way to protect her is to die for her. He also describes how in his time cow-protection had degenerated into a perpetual feud with the Mussulmans. He notes that it is a denial of Hinduism to kill a human being to protect a cow. In his view, cow-protection means 'conquering Mussulmans by our love'. Gandhi also provides the details of 'inhumanities' and 'ill-treats' practiced by Hindus on the cow and her progeny and terms it as 'crime' against the speechless creature. He writes that 'by every act of cruelty to our cattle, we disown God and Hinduism'. He laments that the condition of cattle in any other part of the world is not 'so bad as in unhappy India'. 'We may not blame the Englishman for this. We may not plead poverty in our defense'. Thus he writes, 'Whilst professing the religion of cow-protection, we have enslaved the cow and her progeny, and have become slaves ourselves' (*ibid.*, 249).

He focuses on his fourth point, idol-worship. He writes, 'I know the vice that is going on today in all the great Hindu shrines, but I love them in spite of their unspeakable failings.' He states that he is 'a reformer through and through' but his 'zeal never takes him to the rejection of any of the essential things of Hinduism' (*ibid.*, 249). He notes that he does not disbelieve in idol-worship, although an idol does not 'excite any feeling of veneration' in him. However, he finds that idol worship is part of human nature. Human beings hanker after symbolism thus 'images are an aid to worship' (*ibid.*, 249). On this basis, he does not consider idol-worship a sin.

In the final section of his article, he summarizes his arguments. He notes that Hinduism is not an exclusive religion and in it, there is room for the worship of all the prophets of the world. Moreover, Hinduism is 'not a missionary religion' in the ordinary sense of the term. He notes that Hinduism has absorbed many tribes in its fold, but this absorption has been of an evolutionary imperceptible character. Further, 'Hinduism tells everyone to worship God according to his own faith or *dharma*, and so it lives at peace with all the religions'. He argues that having such a conception of Hinduism, he has never been able to reconcile himself to untouchability. He regarded the untouchability as 'an excrescence' (*ibid.*, 250).

Besides untouchability, Gandhi criticizes the system of *Devdasi* as a part of Hinduism practiced by Hindus in many parts of India. Further, he viewed goat sacrifices to Kali as 'positive irreligious' and did not consider it as part of Hinduism. Also, he outlines his theory of Hinduism, pointing out that it is a product of many ages. In his words, "The very name, Hinduism, was given to the religion of the people of Hindustan by foreigners. There was no doubt at the one-time sacrifice of animals offered in the name of religion. But it is not a religion, much less is it Hindu religion. And so also it seems to me, that when cow-protection became an article of faith with our ancestors, those who persisted in eating beef were excommunicated. The civil strife must have been fierce. Social boycott was applied not only to the recalcitrants, but their sins were visited upon their children also. The practice which had probably its origin in good intentions hardened into usage, and even verses crept in our sacred books giving the practice a permanence wholly undeserved and still less justified" (*ibid.*, 250). Offering this theory of Hinduism, Gandhi returns to the question of untouchability in Hinduism. He finally claims that "Whether my theory is correct or not, untouchability is repugnant to reason and to the instinct of mercy, pity or love. A religion that establishes the worship of the cow cannot possibly countenance or warrant a cruel and inhuman boycott of human beings. And I should be content to be torn to pieces rather than disown the suppressed classes. Hindus will certainly never deserve freedom, nor get it if they allow their noble religion to be disgraced by the retention of the taint of untouchability. And as I love Hinduism dearer than life itself, the taint has become for me an intolerable burden. Let us not deny God by denying to a fifth of our race the right of the association on an equal footing" (CWMG 21: 250).

NOTE

1. The Collected Works of Mahatma Gandhi (CWMG Vol. 1-100) is a standard source of Gandhi's writings and speeches. This one-time authentic documentation of Gandhi's available writings was carried out meticulously, and conscientiously under the CWMG project of the Government of India in 1956. The author has used the CWMG-KS-1956-1994 edition for this book. Retrived from *https://www.gandhiheritageportal.org/. CWMG Vol.1-100.*

REFERENCE

Gandhi. M.K. (2015). *An Autobiography or The Story of my experiments with truth*. Ahmedabad: Navajivan.

2
Hinduism and Humiliation
Ambedkar's *Waiting for a Visa*

Though I am born as Hindu, I will not die as Hindu.
(Ambedkar, Yeola, 13 October, 1935)

Dr. B.R. Ambedkar (1891-1956), the pioneering social reformer of India, is known for his brutal critique of Hinduism. He also publicly denounced untouchability prevailed in Hinduism by burning the *Manusmriti* – a sacred scripture of Hindu religion. It is not widely known that he was so disappointed by the prevailing system of untouchability that he declared to renounce Hinduism in 1936. The year 1956 saw him formally accept Buddhism as well. Having grown up in an untouchable but religious Hindu family, Ambedkar's final rejection of Hinduism reveals the long trauma of untouchability. It is worthwhile mentioning that Hinduism was not rejected by Ambedkar on the basis of an emotional reaction, but by his long-term experience and logical analysis of it. We will discuss his critique of Hinduism through his text *Waiting for a Visa* in the current chapter.[1]

The text *Waiting for a Visa* is a direct narrative of his life. It exposes his frustration with what he sees as the outdated ideologies and customs of Hinduism, which bind his caste status to social inequality. This slim volume is one of the very few books that Ambedkar wrote about himself. It appears to have been written in the year 1935-36. In this short memoir, he describes his agony and struggles as an untouchable. It is entirely different in style and content from everything else he wrote. Its content describes a series of incidents that happened regularly during his life. Also, he illustrates how the humiliation of untouchability, a feature of the Hindu religion, shattered his anticipations and a sense of accomplishment. It painfully informs how inescapable untouchability is for someone born as a Dalit. It offers a view, in short, why Ambedkar was against the Hindu religion. The text can also be viewed as the social pathology of the Hindu religion.[2] Besides this text, we will also touch upon his biography, authored by Dhananjay Keer. This will supplement and substantiate the subtext of his writings in *Waiting for a Visa*.

As a text, *Waiting for a Visa* goes beyond Ambedkar's autobiography. It also reveals the intimate stories of other Dalit individuals. In this sense, it becomes the story of an untouchable community rather than the individual accounts. In addition to highlighting discrimination, it also refers to acts of resistance against the practice of untouchability. Further, it speaks to Ambedkar's desire for Dalits to be empowered.[3] In a way, it also challenges the ongoing prejudices of caste Hindus. It makes them think and question their casteist way of life and beliefs.[4] The title '*Waiting for a Visa*' gives an excellent sense of the content of the book. It portrays Ambedkar's longing for the Hindu religion to sanction his identity, which he never received.

What does *Waiting for a Visa* mean? The title is metaphorical. 'Waiting' in the title refers to Dalits' generational and lifelong wait for justice and equality. Their hope is to enter the 'other space' where they can find freedom and recognition. Indirectly, the term also refers to the 'specific situation' that still forbids untouchables from entering any other 'space'. It confines and keeps them imprisoned in a rigid space of exploitation and oppression. 'Visa' in the title implies a desire to leave the space of untouchability and move into a space marked by freedom and equality. The title *Waiting for a Visa*, thus, signifies how the untouchable Dalit community is still waiting to be accepted by Hindu society as a whole. Ambedkar harbours hope of such an entry despite the strong conviction that this is not going to happen. The title, *Waiting for a Visa*, also reflects the tension and fear inherent in the situation. This makes the book a valuable resource for understanding the exploitation and oppression of India's untouchables, as well as Ambedkar's critique of Hinduism.

Structurally the text comprises a very brief introductory passage followed by six sections; relating Ambedkar's experiences with untouchability, starting from his childhood. Sections 1, 2, 3 and 4 consist of his own experiences, while Sections 5 and 6 consist of other people's experiences with untouchability.

Reading *Waiting for a Visa*

Ambedkar begins his booklet with a short one-paragraph introduction designed for foreign learners and anyone who is unfamiliar with the concept of untouchability.

"Foreigners of course know of the existence of untouchability. But not being next door to it, so to say, they are unable to realise how oppressive it is in its actuality. It is difficult for them to understand how it is possible for a few untouchables to live on the edge of a village consisting of a large number of Hindus; go through the village daily to free it from the most disagreeable of its filth and to carry the errands of all and sundry; collect food at the doors of the Hindus; buy spices and oil at the shops of the Hindu Bania from a distance; regard the village in every way as their home—and yet never touch or be touched by anyone belonging to the village" (Ambedkar, 2017: 158).

Ambedkar clearly observes that being aware of the existence of untouchability and being untouchable are quite two different matters. He raises the question of a difference between the knower of the subject and being itself the subject. 'To know' is superficial and does not represent reality, especially in the context of untouchability. Knowing is a mental exercise, while being is the question of existence. Just knowing that untouchability exists is not enough to truly comprehend its oppression. Ambedkar actually informs us about the social pattern of Hindu religion, which is beyond the scope of human reasoning. Further, untouchability is a condition of remaining part of the Hindu religious system yet outside of it. He tells us through some examples how an untouchable is part of a village, serves the caste Hindus, but never touches them or is touched by them. The agony is that one is completely part of a system, but the system rejects it and not only undermines its role, but also humiliates it. For untouchables, their village is home yet they don't belong to it. One cannot comprehend this pain until one is born untouchable.

Ambedkar also observes the problem of depicting untouchability to others. He informs us that there are two ways to deal with it. The first is to list a general description of untouchability, the second is to record the cases of untouchability and the treatment they received. He seems to be making a difference between what is called the 'author of experience' and the 'owner of the experience'. For him, being an author of experience does not capture the agony the Dalits feel. This can also be seen as a critique of abstractionism, especially if the real situation has to be portrayed. Ambedkar uses the second method of recording cases and treatment to make his point. He notes, "I have felt that the latter would be more effective than the former. In choosing these illustrations I have drawn partly upon my experience and partly upon the experience of others. I begin with events that have happened to me in my own life" (Ambedkar, 2017: 158).

I

'Our family came originally from Dapoli Taluka of the Ratnagiri District of the Bombay Presidency. From the very commencement of the rule of the East India Company my forefathers had left their hereditary occupation for service in the Army of the Company. My father also followed the family tradition and sought service in the Army' (Ambedkar, 2017: 158). By using the term following 'family tradition' Ambedkar is pointing out something very deeper. As Keer in his biography notes, "The family belonged to the devotional Kabir School of Thought, found consolation in the human attributes like compassion, benevolence and resignation to God. These devotees sought moral and spiritual food in Lord Krishna or Shri Rama. But the most humanising and broadening effect upon their mind was that the followers of this Bhakti school had abolished the rigidity of the caste system as Kabir, the founder of the school had condemned it" (Keer, 2013: 8). Keer also points out that Ramji Sakpal, Ambedkar's father lived a very 'industrious and intensely religious life'. His mother Bhimabai was a 'pious, gentle and self-respecting woman' (*ibid.*, 10). She came from a rich family and also belonged to the Kabir cult. His father also took a keen interest in 'religious and theological discussions'. He offered prayers and devotion to God, morning and evening. He read and recited to his children the great national epics, the *Ramayana* and the *Mahabharat*. He also sang spiritual songs of Moropant, Mukteswar and Tukaram. The constant recitals, recitations, and exposition of these songs provided the children with a certain toning and command of the language in their early age. Ramji Sakpal knew the importance of education in his life. He always wanted to help his children to be emancipated from the society which followed casteism rigidly. He had seen and 'undergone discrimination as he belonged to this group, however, he never wanted his children to experience these hardships' (*ibid.*, 11-12).

In contrast, his children had to endure discrimination and humiliation since childhood. The first section of *Waiting for a Visa* describes a journey undertaken in 1901 by the ten-year-old Ambedkar and his siblings, from their residence in Satara to Koregaon, to meet their father. During the journey they faced discriminatory behaviour and humiliation because of their untouchable status and it made a lasting impact on Ambedkar. He writes,

> "The first incident which I am recording as well as I can remember, occurred in about 1901 when we were at Satara. We were well dressed children. From our dress or talk, no one could make out

that we were children of the untouchables. Indeed the station-master was quite sure we were Brahmin children and was extremely touched at the plight in which he found us. As is usual among the Hindus the station-master asked us who we were. Without a moment's thought I blurted out that we were Mahars. (Mahar is one of the communities which are treated as untouchables in the Bombay Presidency). He was stunned. His face underwent a sudden change. We could see that he was overpowered by a strange feeling of repulsion. ...This incident has a very important place in my life. I was a boy of nine when it happened. But it has left an indelible impression on my mind. Before this incident occurred, I knew that I was an untouchable and that untouchables were subjected to certain indignities and discriminations. For instance, I knew that in the school I could not sit in the midst of my class students according to my rank but that I was to sit in a corner by myself. I knew that in the school I was to have a separate piece of gunny cloth for me to squat on in the classroom and the servant employed to clean the school would not touch the gunny cloth used by me. I was required to carry the gunny cloth home in the evening and bring it back the next day. While in the school I knew that children of the touchable classes, when they felt thirsty, could go out to the water tap, open it and quench their thirst. All that was necessary was the permission of the teacher. But my position was separate. I could not touch the tap and unless it was opened for it by a touchable person, it was not possible for me to quench my thirst. In my case the permission of the teacher was not enough. The presence of the school peon was necessary, for, he was the only person whom the class teacher could use for such a purpose. If the peon was not available I had to go without water. The situation can be summed up in the statement—no peon, no water. At home I knew that the work of washing clothes was done by my sisters. Not that there were no washermen in Satara. Not that we could not afford to pay the washermen. Washing was done by my sisters because we were untouchables and no washerman would wash the clothes of an untouchable. The work of cutting our hair or shaving the boys, including myself, was done by our elder sister, who had become quite an expert barber by practising the art on us. Not that there were no barber in Satara, and not that we could not afford to pay the barber. The work of shaving and hair-cutting was done by my sister because we were untouchables, and no barber would consent to shave an untouchable. All this I knew. But this

> incident gave me a shock such as I had never received before, and it made me think about untouchability—which, before this incident happened, was with me a matter of course, as it is with many touchables as well as the untouchables" (Ambdakar, 2017: 159-166).

But this was not the first and last experience. Keer in his biography records the number of humiliations that Ambedkar faced during his childhood and school days. In school, he was made to sit on the floor far away from other students. He was not allowed to go close to the blackboard as other students would place their lunch boxes near the board. Getting near the blackboard meant polluting the foodstuff, in which case, the other students would have to become hungry. He had to sit outside the classroom and teachers would not touch him or his books as they believed it would pollute them. As a little boy one rainy day, he was totally drenched while heading to school since he could not afford an umbrella. Dripping wet he had to sit outside the classroom for the whole day as he wasn't allowed to enter the classroom. Such galling humiliations and inhuman treatment left an indelible mark on his mind and heart. He was also not allowed to take up Sanskrit though he had an eager desire to learn it. This was another 'pill of poison' that was rammed down the unwilling throats of Ambedkar by the defenders of Hinduism (Keer, 2013: 19). Later on, Ambedkar noted, "Sanskrit is the golden treasure of epics, the cradle of grammar, politics, and philosophy and the home of logic, dramas, and criticism" (Keer, 2013: 19). It was a sacrilege for a shudra and that too for an Untouchable to even hear, much less to learn Sanskrit which was the key to the Vedas. He was thus forced to take up Persian as the second language as during that time only the high caste Hindus had the privilege to learn Sanskrit. When he joined the college, he had to face the same humiliation and discrimination. During his college days as a student of Elphinstone College, the College canteen keeper who was a Brahmin would not give him tea or water. Even as a professor at Sydenham College, Bombay he faced the same social ill-treatment. "The High Caste Professors objected to his drinking water from the pot reserved for the staff" (Keer, 2013: 39).

Even after being highly qualified Ambedkar did not get the right treatment from society. In one such phase of his life, he started a business firm offering advice to dealers in stocks and shares. However, as customers were reluctant to ask for advice from an untouchable, he had to close it permanently. All these unpleasant experiences received by him and by his whole community for untold ages engendered in him a 'burning hatred for Hinduism'.

However, when he moved to America in 1913 for higher study, he observed democracy in practice there as he lived with other students on an equal basis. He was also impressed with the American practice of working combined with studying. He observed how this spirit of self-help fostered a feeling of self-respect, confidence, and more active participation in community and National Services. In June 1915, he obtained his Master's degree for his thesis, 'Ancient Indian Commerce' and the thesis was published in May 1917. In May 1916, he read a paper on 'The Caste in India', their Mechanism, Genesis and Development before the Anthropology Seminar of Dr. Goldenweiser. In June 1916, he submitted his thesis for the degree of Ph.D. entitled 'National Dividend of India - A Historic and Analytical Study'. It was published eight years later under the title 'The Evolution of Provincial Finance in British India'. The book was dedicated to Maharaja Sayajirao Gaikwad and had an introduction by Prof. S.A. Selig, the well-known economist from Columbia University. Later on, Ambedkar joined the London School of Economics and Political Science as a post-graduate student in June 1916. In October 1916, he got admitted to the Gray's Inn for Law. However, he had to return to India after spending a year in London working on a thesis for the M.Sc. (Eco) Degree on account of the termination of the scholarship granted to him by Sayajirao Gaikwad.

II

"In 1916, I returned to India. I had been sent to America by His Highness the Maharaja of Baroda for higher education. I studied at Columbia University in New York from 1913 to 1917. In 1917 I came to London and joined the Post-graduate Department of the School of Economics of the University of London. In 1918, I was obliged to return to India without completing my studies. Since I had been educated by the Baroda State, I was bound to serve the State" (Ambedkar 2017: 166).

He further notes, "My five years of staying in Europe and America had completely wiped out of my mind any consciousness that I was an untouchable, and that an untouchable wherever he went in India was a problem to himself and to others' (*ibid.*, 166). One might argue how his five-year stay in Europe and America had completely erased his mind and self-conception that he was untouchable? The answer lies in the influence of European thinking and the influence that shaped his thoughts and mind. Although Ambedkar regarded three prominent Indian men as his preceptors, he was equally influenced by European and American thinkers. Among the three Indian thinkers, the first was Kabir who took him to the Bhakti (devotion) cult. The second was Jyotiba Phule who inspired him to strive for anti-Brahmanism and amelioration of the masses; their education and economic uplift. The third was the Buddha who gave him metaphysical satisfaction and showed the way leading to the emancipation of the untouchables, by resorting to the path of mass conversion. Among the American and European intellectuals, he was deeply influenced by the writings and teaching of Prof. John Dewey, who was his teacher at Columbia.[5]

He was particularly impressed by the humanistic approach and liberal attitude of John Dewey. John Dewey's philosophy was meaningful to Ambedkar as it offered the idea that educated and politically aware people could work out their own political destiny in a pragmatic way. His philosophy also provided him insight into 'pruning the useless and preserving the useful' of society. Dewey's philosophy that informed about the problems of the common man gave Ambedkar consolation and inspiration. Ambedkar always felt that man should not conserve the whole of his social heritage but select what is helpful and transmit to future generations only that much and no more. Dewey's influence on Ambedkar can be seen in Ambedkar's writings while he quotes the former, "Every society gets encumbered with what is trivial with dead wood from the past and with what is positively perverse... . As a society becomes more enlightened, it realises that it is responsible not to conserve and transmit the whole of its existing achievements, but only such as make for a better future society" (Ambedkar, Vol. 1., 1979: 79). Quoting the views of John Dewey, Ambedkar shows how the worship of the past in every respect is harmful for the reconstruction of society. This influence indicates how he has exercised this insight to evaluate ancient Hindu texts and Hindu society.

Further, Dewey's philosophy of instrumentalism led Ambedkar towards a critical analysis of the concrete problems facing humanity. His pragmatic approach convinced Ambedkar that philosophy must be dynamic if it seeks to solve the problem of humanity. Dewey criticized the ancient philosophers who advocated idealism and other obsolete things also (Ambedkar, 1955: 34). Similarly, Ambedkar also criticized the ancient philosophers of India like *Kapila* and the religious books known as the *Brahmanas* and *Upanishads*. Here he was influenced by Dewey's method of inquiry which provided a way to deal with painful situations. He was also impressed by Dewey's activist epistemology and the idea of a realist school of political scientists. Therefore, he paid pointed attention to practical rather than mere academic politics. Politics is nothing if not realistic. In order to assess any political scheme, one must first consider the ground plan To him, the ground plan means the social structure of a community to which the political plan is sought to be applied (Ambedkar 1955: 34).

Dewey's concept of instrumentalism had two characteristics—symmetry and cohesiveness. Both appealed to the young mind of Ambedkar. Dewey's ideas provided the basis for a systematic analysis of problems relating to politics, economics, society, religion, and history; however, these problems are interrelated, thus demanding an integral approach to the solution (Ambedkar, 1936: 73).

Ambedkar tried to adapt Dewey's philosophy in Indian context. As one of the scholars has noted, "There is reason to believe that Ambedkar admired and internalized Dewey's ideas of deep democracy, reconstruction, and reflective morality and wove these into the tapestry of reform that his life represented. He was a pragmatist, albeit one with a distinctively Indian concern with the problems and boons of religions in a pluralistic community. Much more can be said about the relationship between Ambedkar the caste reformer and the American pragmatist Dewey, but it is now clear that Dewey's influence can be charted in specific and traceable ways in Ambedkar's writings, speeches, and activities. Like Dewey, Ambedkar was firmly committed to achieving equality, liberty and fraternity; unlike Dewey, he had the traditional materials and imaginative resources to see Buddhism as the religious means that could be reconstructed and used for these meliorative ends. It is in acknowledging this debt and foundation that we can start to appreciate what Ambedkar does with American pragmatism when he adapts it to the Indian context."[6] The second person who influenced him was William Garrison. He had formed the first abolitionist society in favour of the immediate freeing of all slaves. He worked for the emancipation of Negro slaves and fought for their civil liberty. Through his newspaper 'Liberator' he created public opinion in favour of the liberation of the Nigroes.[7] Influenced by him, Ambedkar relentlessly reminded the caste Hindus that the deadly disease of Casteism required drastic measures. This disease which is deep-rooted in Indian society will not be cured simply by dressing with a bandage of knowledge or even the paper scheme would not cure it. To quote Ambedkar, "Dragging on life somehow or to live like a crow for a thousand years is not the only and worthy way to live in this world. Life can be ennobled and immortalized by sacrificing it for lasting good, such as the cause of truth, a vow, honour, or country. For the protection of human rights several great men have immolated themselves at the altar of duty" (Keer, 1954: 91). In this statement, Ambedkar confirms his commitment to freeing his brethren from the clutches of the high caste Hindus. The third person who influenced Ambedkar's intellectual development was J.S. Mill. From Mill's writings, Ambedkar got the importance of individuals' initiative and personal responsibility. Like Mill, Ambedkar was also convinced that freedom of thought is indispensable although freedom of action may be limited.[8]

The second section of *Waiting for a Visa* can be read keeping these influences in mind. His mindset was full of these ideas when he came back from America and London and reached Baroda in 1918. But as he reached Baroda state to work as a probationer in the Accountant General's Office, he again felt the agony of being untouchable. He realized that none of the Hindu hotels would allow him to stay due to his lower caste. "I had friends in Baroda who had come to America for study. 'Would they welcome me if I went?' I could not assure myself. They may feel embarrassed at admitting an untouchable into their household. I stood under the roof of the station for some time, thinking where to go, what to do" (Ambedkar, 2017: 168).

The section 2 of the text describes the deep divides that existed in Baroda during that time, not just between castes, but also between religions. He found a Parsi inn, but here, non-Parsis were not allowed to stay. He and the Parsi innkeeper reached a compromise, whereby Ambedkar gave his name as a Parsi and was allowed to stay. However, this fraud (his words) was discovered by other Parsis, and on the eleventh day of his stay, a group of angry Parsi men, armed with sticks, arrived to remove him from the inn. He had to leave the inn that very day, and not having a place to stay, was forced to leave Baroda and return to Bombay to find work elsewhere. "This scene of a dozen Parsis armed with sticks lined [up] before me in a menacing mood, and myself standing before them with a terrified look imploring for mercy, is a scene which so long a period as eighteen years has not succeeded in fading away. I can even now vividly recall it—and [I] never recall it without tears in my eyes. It was then for the first time that I learnt that a person who is an untouchable to a Hindu is also an untouchable to a Parsi" (Ambedkar, 2017: 174).

III

In the third section, Ambedkar recounts an embarrassing accident that occurred to him in the village of Chalisgaon (Maharashtra) in 1929. He had been appointed as a member to a committee instituted by the Bombay government, to investigate allegations of oppression and grievances of untouchables. After carrying out investigations in the district of

Khandesh, *en route* to Bombay, he disembarked at Chalisgaon to investigate a case of the social boycott by Hindus against untouchables of that village. The untouchables of the village requested him to spend the night with them, but as the *tongawallas* considered it below their dignity to cart an untouchable (Ambedkar), the villagers had to hire a *tonga* (horse-driven carriage) and ride it on their own. They did so, however the untouchable riding the carriage was a novice, and had an accident as they were crossing the river on a culvert. Ambedkar was thrown off the carriage as a wheel got stuck between the stones of the culvert. This resulted in multiple injuries to Ambedkar and a fracture. The horse and carriage fell into the river. Ambedkar feels that the pride and dignity of the village untouchables, as they did not want their visitor to have to walk to the village, made them take undue risks with the safety of their visitor. He also realized that even lowly menial *tongawallas* felt that even a highly educated Barrister-at-Law if he is untouchable is below them. He concludes the section by stating, "To save my dignity, the Mahars of Chalisgaon had put my very life in jeopardy. It is then I learnt that a Hindu *tongawalla*, no better than a menial, has a dignity by which he can look upon himself as a person who is superior to any untouchable, even though he may be a Barrister-at-law" (Ambedkar, 2017: 177).

IV

Section four of *Waiting for a Visa* relates to an incident in 1934 and shows how Muslims also treated untouchables as lower caste. Ambedkar and a group of his friends had gone to visit Daulatabad fort, during a trip to Aurangabad, then in the Nizam state of Hyderabad. On arriving at the fort, Ambedkar's group washed themselves with water kept in a tank at the fort entrance. However, after a few minutes, an old Mohammedan started to run after them, shouting "the Dheds (untouchables) have polluted our water" and soon there was a commotion, with a large group of Muslims shooting at Ambedkar's group and at the local untouchable community. A riot nearly resulted till Ambedkar asked them whether they would have behaved in the same manner if an untouchable who had converted to Islam had used that water. It informs us how Muslims also consider Dalits as untouchable.

V

Section V of the text consists of a letter that was published in *Young India,* a journal published by M.K. Gandhi in its issue of 12 December, 1929. It recounts the sad experience of a *Harijan* in Kathiawar. His wife fell sick soon after giving birth to a child. The Hindu (Brahmin) doctor refused to treat her directly or see them in the house. The doctor finally agreed to see the sick lady if she was brought outside the Harijan colony, and treated here without touching her, by passing the thermometer indirectly through a Muslim. Some medicine was given to her, and when her condition aggravated, the doctor refused to see her. She died subsequently.

The letter mentions.

> "On the 5th of this month, a child was born to me. On the 7th, she [the writer's wife] fell ill and suffered from loose stools. Her vitality seemed to ebb away and her chest became inflamed. Her breathing became difficult and there was acute pain in the ribs. I went to call a doctor—but he said he would not go to the house of a Harijan, nor was he prepared to examine the child. Then I went to [the] Nagarseth and Garasia Darbar and pleaded [with] them to help me. The Nagarseth stood surety to the doctor for my paying his fee of two rupees. Then the doctor came, but on condition that he would examine them only outside the Harijan colony. I took my wife out of the colony along with her newly born child. Then the doctor gave his thermometer to a Muslim, he gave it to me, and I gave it to my wife and then returned it by the same process after it had been applied. It was about eight o'clock in the evening and the doctor, on looking at the thermometer in the light of a lamp, said that the patient was suffering from pneumonia. Then the doctor went away and sent the medicine. I brought some linseed from the bazar and used it on the patient. The doctor refused to see her later, although I gave the two rupees fee. The disease is dangerous and God alone will help us. The lamp of my life has died out. She passed away at about two o'clock this afternoon" (Ambedkar, 2017, 180-181).

Ambedkar writes, "No explanation is necessary. The doctor, in spite of being educated, refused to apply the thermometer and treat an ailing woman in a critical condition. As a result of his refusal to treat her, the woman died. He felt no qualms of conscience in setting aside the code of conduct which is binding on his profession. The Hindu would prefer to be inhuman rather than touch an Untouchable." (*ibid.*, 181)

VI

Section VI recounts the narrated experience of a Bhangi boy, recounted on 6 March, 1938 at a Bhangi meeting in Dadar, Bombay. The educated boy got employment as a Talati in the government district offices of Borsad, Kheda (now in Gujarat). However, he was refused accommodation there, being untouchable. Neither did the untouchables of the village accommodate him, fearing the wrath of Hindus who felt that the bhangi boy was aiming for a job that was beyond him. At the government office, his colleagues discriminated against him, treated him badly, and did not allow him to drink water when thirsty for fear of the water getting polluted by his touch. Ultimately, matters only got worse, with a large crowd of locals threatening to kill him. He left this job and returned home.

In short, divided into six sections Ambedkar narrates different experiences of humiliation and discrimination because of untouchability in the Hindu religion. The text describes his struggles both as a child as well as an adult to achieve basic yet indispensable things like water, shelter, food, travel, medical assistance and to some extent education and a job too. The author tries to emphasize the untouchable's desire for these amenities. The discrimination he experienced also left a lasting impression on him. As a text, his narration compels the readers to visualize the pain and humiliation felt by him because of untouchability. The social structure of Hinduism is laid bear with sincerity.

The text is not only a personal record but also the experience of an untouchable community. Although he talks about specific cases of discrimination, he also offers a general overview. In a sense, it is singular in experience but the impact is general.

Waiting for a Visa also questions the role of education in eradicating untouchability. While education has been an effective tool for Ambedkar to challenge the caste Hindu society, we note the disappointments that Dalits experience even after pursuing quality degrees and getting prestigious jobs. On the other hand, in some cases, Ambedkar shows that many 'well-educated' caste Hindus would rather risk the lives of their 'untouchable' patients than come in close contact with them. From these experiences Ambedkar concluded that the problem lies not in the people but in the Hindu religion and its philosophy itself.

Ambedkar's views on Hinduism and the emancipation of untouchables are closely related. However, it was not homogeneous. As Pantham points out, "Broadly speaking, there were two distinct phases in the strategy and tactics which Ambedkar actually followed for the emancipation of the untouchables from their oppressive and humiliating situation" (Pantham, 2009: 186). In the first phase, he notes, it was roughly till the end of 1934, Ambedkar sought to gain, for the Depressed Classes, equality within Hinduism by trying to reform it through non-violent direct actions by the untouchables themselves. This may be called emancipation through the 'reform of Hinduism'. Recall, it was the opposite of Gandhi's method which called for penitential actions on the part of caste Hindus to eliminate untouchability. In the second phase, from 1935 onwards, Ambedkar, while continuing to demand emancipatory and welfare measures from the government, redefined the primary objective of the movement of the Depressed Classes. It was during this phase that he sought social equality based on the 'Liberation from Hinduism'.

Pantham quotes Ambedkar to explain the difference between these two phases,

> "I thought for long that we could rid the Hindu society of its evils and get the Depressed Classes incorporated into it on terms of equality. That motive inspired the Mahad Chaudar (Water) Tank Satyagraha and the Nasik temple Entry Satyagraha. With that object in mind, we burned the *Manu Smriti* and performed mass thread ceremonies. Experience has taught me better. I stand today absolutely convinced that for the depressed classes there can be no equality among the Hindus because on inequality rest the foundations of Hinduism. We no longer want to be part of the Hindu society" (qtd. in Pantham, 2009: 186). The reform of Hinduism, for a dignified place of untouchables, was to go with the three-fold process of purification of untouchables. Ambedkar said, "We must improve the general tone of our demeanor, re-tone our pronunciations, and revitalize our thoughts. I, therefore ask you now to take a vow from this moment to renounce eating carrion... . Make an unflinching resolve not to eat the throw-our crumbs. We will attain self-elevation only if we learn self-help, regain our self-respect, and gain self-knowledge" (*ibid*., 188). Ambedkar also launched Satyagraha like Gandhi for the emancipation of untouchables. Mahad Satyagraha might be remembered here.[9] During this satyagraha he gave his historic presidential address, in which he said, "The Hindu community is set in the steel frame of Caste system in which one caste is lower than another in social gradation involving particular privileges, rights, inhibitions, and disabilities with regard to each caste. This system has created vested interests which depend upon maintaining the inequalities resulting from the system…" (qtd. in Pantham, 2009: 188)

Finally, it will not be out of context to discuss, in brief, the Kalaram Temple Satyagraha (March 1930). In this satyagraha, he played a leading role and campaigned against the exclusion of the untouchables from the Kalaram Temple at Nasik. It is important to note, after launching the campaign, he did not continue to be personally active in it. He felt that the limited objective of the temple entry movement, namely, to conscientize and energize the depressed classes, had already been achieved. Thus, henceforth they should 'concentrate their energy and resources on politics and education.' Ambedkar believed that social equality is a bigger goal than getting access to the temples and that for the former Hinduism needed to be purged of the doctrine of chaturvarna. But by 1935, when he wrote *Annihilation of Caste*, he was convinced that within Hinduism it is not possible to liberate the untouchables. Soon Ambedkar declared that he would not die as a Hindu and started thinking to leave Hinduism. It took almost 20 years when he formally left Hinduism in 1956.[10]

This is the context in which Ambedkar viewed Hinduism and not only severely criticised, but also negated it.

NOTES

1. *Waiting for a Visa* is his memoir. In 1990, the People's Education Society published this work as a booklet. It was subsequently published by the Education Department, Government of Maharashtra, in 1993 along with some collections in Dr. Babasaheb Ambedkar: Writings and Speeches, Vol. 12, Part I. In this chapter, I have used the text *Waiting for a Visa* published in *Ambedkar The Attendant Details* (2017), Yusufji, Salim (ed.), New Delhi: Navayana.
   It must be reminded that Ambedkar, popularly known as Baba Saheb, was an Indian jurist, politician, and social reformer and campaigned against social discrimination in India. He was striving for equal social rights for Dalits, women, and labour. He was also independent India's first Law Minister and the principal architect of the Constitution of India.
2. Ambedkar believed that Hinduism is caste oriented and caste bound. For him, Caste determines one's station and stature in society. Indian society is a gradation of castes forming an ascending scale of reverence and a descending scale of contempt. The caste system is not just a division of labour but also a hierarchical division of labourers which is not based on natural aptitude or spontaneity but on the caste of parents. Ambedkar terms caste system to be 'Graded Inequality'. He held the view that the caste system could not have been imposed by the Brahmins on society, but it took shape when they were able to persuade other groups that their values were universally superior and that they had to be emulated by

others. According to him, the real line of cleavage among Hindus was not set between Brahmins and Non-Brahmins but between Touchables and Untouchables. Thus, he spent his entire life fighting against the caste system, his sole aim being 'reconstruction of the society'.

3. *Waiting for a Visa* was, in a sense, written to empower Dalits also. Empowering Dalits was his main agenda. In this regard, a brief chronology of his social-political action to uplift the Dalits may be summarized as follows. In 1920, on 31 January, with the help of Dattoba Powar, Ambedkar launched *Mook Nayak* (Leader of the Dumb) newspaper. He was not its official editor, but he was the man behind it, and it was his mouthpiece. Nandram Bhatkar was the editor and later Dyander Gholap succeeded him. In March 1920 he presided over a conference of Untouchables, in Mangaon in Kolhapur state. Shahuji Maharaj was in attendance too. In May 1920, he attended the first All-India Conference convened by Untouchables and presided over by Shahuji Maharaj of Kolhapur. In July 1924, he launched the *Bahishkrit Hitakarini Sabha* (Group for the Wellbeing of the Excluded), to mobilize Depressed Classes. Its motto was "Educate, Agitate, Organise". Ambedkar was the chairman of the managing committee.In 1926, he led the satyagraha in Mahad to secure the right of Untouchables to draw water from the Chavdar Tank. He ceremonially took a drink of water from the tank, after which local caste Hindus run riot, and Brahmins took elaborate measures for the ritual purification of the tank. In 1926, he successfully defended three non-brahmin leaders who had accused the Brahmin community of ruining India and were then subsequently sued for libel. In1927, on 3 April, he launched his Marathi fortnightly *Bahishkrit Bharat*. He himself was the editor. In September 1927, he founded "Samaj Samata Sangh". In 1929, he closed his second journal, *Bahiskrit Bharat* ("Excluded India"), and replaced it with *Janata* ("The People"). In March 1930, he led a satyagraha at the Kalaram Temple in Nasik to secure for Untouchables the right of entry into the temple. On August 8, 1930, he presided over the Depressed Classes Congress in Nagpur and delivered a speech favouring Dominion status. In 1932, Ambedkar was invited to attend the Second Round Table Conference in London. He recommended, "either to reserve seats for those minorities that cannot, otherwise, secure personal representation or grant communal electorates." So he demanded separate electorates, the guarantee of representation, a toll tax for Dalit villages, and Dalit approval for the constitution. Gandhi was against separate electorates for untouchables. When the British agreed, Gandhi protested by fasting in Yerwada jail. Ambedkar criticized Gandhi's fast unto death as a 'political stunt'. When Ambedkar went to meet Gandhi, the latter said, "I know you are a patriot of sterling worth. You are untouchable by birth and I am by adoption." On 23 September, 1932, though very reluctant, he accepted joint electorates, with Gandhi fasting unto death in Yerwada jail, Poona, against the separate electorates granted to the Depressed Classes by Ramsay MacDonald's

Communal Award. The result was the Poona Pact. This also led to the Eternal battle between Ambedkar and Gandhi. On October 13, 1935, he presided over the Yeola Conversion Conference, held in Yeola, in Nashik district. He advised the Depressed Classes to abandon all agitation for temple-entry privileges; instead, he says, they should leave Hinduism entirely and embrace another religion. He vowed, "I solemnly assure you that I will not die as a Hindu." On February 29, 1935, his conversion resolution was supported by the Chambers of East Khandesh. On 13-14 April, he addressed the Sikh Mission Conference in Amritsar and reiterated this intention of renouncing Hinduism.In late April, the Jat-Pat-Todak Mandal withdrew its invitation to him to deliver the presidential address at the Mandal's annual conference in Lahore, after reading the text of his speech. On 15 May, he published the speech text, with an introductory account of the whole controversy. The result was the *Annihilation of Caste*. In 1937, he published the second edition of *The Annihilation of Caste*, adding a concluding appendix that features a debate with Gandhi over the speech text. In 1938, in January, Congress introduced a bill for the amendment of the Local Boards Act in which the Untouchables are defined as Harijans, i.e. sons of God. Ambedkar criticized the nomenclature as in his opinion the change of name would make no real change in their condition. He was against the use of this word in legal matters. In protest of this Bill, the Labour Party members walked out of the assembly. In 1942, he founded his second political party, the All India Scheduled Castes Federation, which went on to perform poorly in the 1946 elections. In 1944, on 29 January, he presided over the second meeting of the All India Scheduled Castes Federation, in Kanpur. On May 6, 1944, he addressed the annual conference of the All-India Scheduled Castes Federation at Parel, in Mumbai. In1951, he introduced in Parliament the Hindu Code Bill that he drafted to enhance the rights of women; it proved very controversial, and consideration of the Bill is postponed. In July, he founded Bhartiya Buddha Jan Sangh. In 1954, while dedicating a new Buddhist Vihara near Pune, he announced that he is writing a book on Buddhism and that as soon as it is finished, he will formally convert to Buddhism. He also claimed that the image of Vithoba at Pandharpur is actually an image of the Buddha, and said that he would write a thesis to prove this claim. In 1955, he founded the Bharatiya Baudh Mahasabha. On 14 October, 1956, his formal conversion took place in Nagpur.

4. It is worth mentioning, for Ambedkar, Brhamisnim and capitalism are two enemies. By the former, he stated, "I do not mean the power, privileges, and interests of the Brahmins as a community. By Brahmanism I mean the negation of the spirit of liberty, equality and fraternity. In that sense, it is rampant in all classes and is not confined to Brahmins alone though they have been its originators" [see, *The History of Social Movements in Global Perspective: A Survey* (2017), edited by Stefan Berger, Holger Nehring, London: Palgrave and Macmillan, p. 283d)].

He asked the untouchable worker to compare the opportunities of their class with those of a touchable and said that the former had fewer opportunities of obtaining work, securing service, or advancement in his respective occupation.

5. In the 1930s, Ambedkar wrote, "The best friends I have had in my life were some of my classmates at Columbia and my great professors, John Dewey, James Shotwell, Edwin Seligman, and James Harvey Robinson" (see *Columbia Alumni News*, 19 December, 1930, 12). Eleanor Zelliot also notes that "John Dewey seems to have had the greatest influence on Ambedkar" (see, Eleanor Zelliot, (2013) *Ambedkar's World*. New Delhi: Navayana, p. 69).
6. https://www.forwardpress.in/2017/05/john-dewey-pragmatism-communication-and-bhimrao-ambedkar
7. Ambedkar has referred to Garrison's view in a number of his speeches and writings directly or indirectly; especially the following view, that occurred in the first issue of '*Liberator*'. 'I shall strenuously contend for the immediate enforcement of our slave population... . On this subject, I do not wish to write or speak or think with moderation. No, No tell a man whose house is on fire to give a moderate alarm. Tell him to moderately rescue his wife from the hands of the ravisher. Tell the mother to gradually extricate her babe from the fire into which it has fallen, but urge me not into moderation in a cause like the present. I am earnest—1 will not excuse—I will not retreat a single inch and I will be heard" (see, Editorial in the Liberator, Vol. 1 by Garrison in Sage, American history.net.html).
8. He said the liberty of the individual should be limited as it can become a nuisance to the other. This idea he expressed in a forceful statement before the Constituent Assembly while dealing with the exceptions and qualifications of the Fundamental Rights.
9. For this satyagraha, Ambedkar organized a series of the public meetings in Bombay and publicized the issue in the Press. The orthodox Hindus filed a civil suit claiming the tank to be their private property and obtained, on 14 December, 1927, a temporary injunction preventing the untouchables' access to the tank Undeterred. Ambedkar and his followers organized a conference at Mahad on 25 December, 1927 for launching a satyagraha. At the inaugural session, in a pavilion featuring Gandhi's photo, which was attended, among others, by several prominent Hindu social reformers as well as by the District Collector and the District Superintendent of Police. (See Annexure II for his Historic Speech during Mahad Agitation).
10. His conversion is highly illuminating. In a broadcast in May 1956 on BBC on 'Why I like Buddhism and how it is useful to the world in its present circumstances', he said, I prefer Buddhism because it gives three principles that no other religion gives, one it teaches *prajna* (understanding as against superstition and super nationalism), *karuna* (love), and *samata* (equality). This is what man wants for a good and happy life. Marxism and Communism have shaken the religious system of all countries. Buddhist countries that

have gone into communism do not understand what communism is'. On 24/5/1956, at a talk in Nare Park, Bombay he declared that he would embrace Buddhism in October 1956. In his speech, he attacked Savarkar who had written a series of articles on the non-violence preached by Buddhism. To him, Buddhism differed from Hinduism. Hinduism believed in God and soul the former did not. Hinduism believed in Chaturvarna and the caste system the former did not. During his speech, Ambedkar compared himself with Moses who had led his people from Egypt to Palestine, the land of freedom. On September 23, he issued a press note announcing that his conversion to Buddhism would take place at Nagpur on Dassara day on 14/10/1956 between 9 and 11 a.m. He wrote to D. Valisinha expressing the desire that Mahabodhi Society of India should participate in the function. He informed him that he had no idea what the rituals were although he had framed an important formula of a series of vows to be administered at the time of the Dhamma Diksha Ceremony. He said that his Buddhism would be a sort of neo-Buddhism or Navayana. He declared that he had once told Gandhi, although he differed from him on the issue of untouchability, when the time came, 'I will choose only the least harmful way for the country. And that is the greatest benefit I am conferring on the country by embracing Buddhism, for Buddhism is a part and parcel of Bharatiya culture. I have taken care that my conversion will not harm the tradition of the culture and history of this land. He predicted that in the next 10-15 years India would become a Buddhist country (see, Keer, 2013: 490-95).

REFERENCES

Ambedkar, B.R. (1936). *Annihilation of Caste.* Bombay: New Books Co.

Ambedkar, B.R. (1955). *Thoughts of Linguistic States*. Aurangabad: Milind Mahavidyalaya.

Ambedkar, B.R. (Vol. I, 1979). *Writings and Speeches.* Government, of Maharashtra.

Ambedkar. B.R. (2017). *Ambedkar The Attendant Details.* Yusufji, Salim (ed.), New Delhi: Navayana.

Keer, Dhananjay (2013). *Dr. Babasaheb Ambedkar*. Bombay: Popular Prakashan.

Pantham, T. (2009). 'Against Untouchability: The Discourse of Gandhi and Ambedkar' in Gopal Guru (ed.) *Humiliation.* New Delhi: Oxford University Press.

3
The Genesis and Evolution of Savarkar's Hindutva

Hindus are the heart of Hindustan .

(Savarkar, qtd. in Sampath 2019, 250)

Vinayak Damodar Savarkar (1883-1966), known as Veer Savarkar, is known for his political construct of Hindutva. His idea of Hindutva, his construct for a Hindu nation, evolved over time and under the influence of a series of historical events. In this chapter, we will examine Savarkar's life and significant events, from his birth to his release from prison in 1923, to understand the genesis and development of Hindutva. As Savarkar did not write his autobiography, we are compelled to view his biographies so as to mark out his life and events that influenced his Hindutva viewpoint. To accomplice this task, we will draw upon his three biographies, *Life of Barrister Savarkar* (1926) by Chitragupta, *Savarkar and his Times* (1950) by Dhananjay Keer, and the recently published *Savarkar Echoes from a Forgotten Past,* Part 1 (2019) by Vikram Sampath.[1] To supplement the details in our present endeavour, we will also draw upon other recent and relevant studies.

Life of Barrister Savarkar (1926, 1987) is the first biography of Savarkar in English. In the preface to the second edition of this book, written by Dr. Ravindra Vaman Ramdas on 26 February, 1926, it is mentioned that 'though many details are lacking, this is the first biography of Veer Savarkar in English' (Chitragupta, 1987: 1). It covers the period of Savarkar's life up to 30th January, 1911, when he was sentenced to second transportation for life. The preface also notes, 'Who was this Chitragupta, the author of Life of Barrister V.D. Savarkar'? The pen-picture of Paris appears that Chitragupta is 'none other than Veer Savarkar' (*ibid.*, 4). But why Savarkar did not disclose it even after Independence will ever remain a 'mystery', the preface mentions (*ibid.*, 5).

Dhananjay Keer's biography *Savarkar and His Times* is the first full-length biography of Savarkar. This biography has been considered as the authoritative source for Savarkar's life, especially the early years. The author notes that he has made 'a faithful attempt to present a true and correct picture of the various events and incidents that occurred in Savarkar's life' (Keer, 1950: v). Although Keer's biography of Savarkar has been criticized by many terming it as a hagiography, yet, it is a full length biography. Recently, Vikram Sampath has written a comprehensive biography of Savarkar. It is divided into two volumes. About his biography, he claims , "Within this rubric of several biographies, this book posits itself as one that presents to its readers an objective assessment of Savarkar and his contemporaries based on extensive archival research of original documents from across the world and hitherto unused Marathi documents" (Sampath, 2019: 25).

I

That emerges from these three books provides some significant clues about Savarkar's life and his ideas. We are informed that Savarkar was a *Chitpavan* Brahmin, a community that had produced Nana Shahib of 1857 fame, Vasudeo Balwant and Tilak. These were people who strove for Independence from the hands of the British. Born in 1883, in the small village of Baghur outside the town of Nasik in Maharashtra, Savarkar's father Damodar was a religious-minded man who kept a strict household. The parents, Damodar and Radhabai, had four children—Ganesh, the oldest; Vinayak, the second; Mainabai, a daughter; and finally, the youngest, Narayan. We are further informed by the biographers that his family was religious. "Growing up in a religious family, with a very pious and devout mother and father, Vinayak was exposed early to such texts as the *Mahabharata* and the *Ramayana*, which were often read aloud in the evenings by Damodar or one of his sons" (Chitragupta, 1987: 15). We are also informed that in his home there existed an old, dirty shelf in a neglected corner. "On it were thrown pell-mell a number of magazines containing translations of *Mahabharat*—several copies out of the files of the famous *Kesari* of Tilak, a well bound volume of Nibandhamala of Chiplunker—the first of the Maratha nationalists, one or two Bhakars chronicling the exploits of the Marathas in their Imperial days. These formed his mental food. He was often found absorbed in ranking, studying and pouring over these files and pages and pathetically inducing his young schoolmates to come and share his intellectual and emotional joys" (*ibid.*, 16).

From his early childhood, Savarkar was familiar with many epic heroes of Hindu culture, especially Shivaji, the Hindu warrior from Maharashtra. Remind that it was Shivaji who first resisted Mughal imperialism in the latter half of the 17th century. All biographers agree it was Shivaji's heroism which provided a source of inspiration and the revolutionary fervour to young Savarkar. We also learn that Vinayak had lofty aspirations since his childhood, as indicated by those who came into contact with him during his childhood. He was recognized as an exceptionally gifted child. Vinayak was entrusted by his father with offering the customary daily worship to the household Gods. There was an imposing and beautifully wrought brass image of Durga around which numerous family traditions and myths revolved. He had read that Durga was the patronizing deity of Shivaji. At her feet he would sit for hours, at times so completely lost in communication as to loose all outward consciousness. He lost his mother when he was ten years old. "...But apart from all that Vinayak especially never missed into mother; for to him the image of Durga had grown into a living and loving and as real a mother as any incorporated human being could be" (*ibid.*, 22).

Certain events shaped Savarkar's childhood mindset. In June 1893, serious Hindu Muslim riots broke out in Azamgarh district in today's Uttar Pradesh and in August the same year in Bombay. The news of atrocities perpetuated on Hindus fired his blood and Savarkar resolved to take revenge. "Savarkar led a batch of selected schoolmates in a march upon the local village mosque, shattered its windows. The Muslims responded but Savarkar with his friends routed the enemies" (Keer, 1950: 4).

The last decade of the nineteenth century was the decade of intense political agitation and awakening in Maharashtra. It was a time when the modern Maratha Power was trying to assert itself. The remarkable sessions of the National Congress at Poona, the social conference controversy, the Shivaji celebrations and the Ganapati festivals, had all roused and worked up the Maratha people as never before. "Vinayak, now about 14, lived and breathed and had his being in this tense political atmosphere" (Chitragupta, 1987: 23).

His curiosity about political events dates back to his childhood. Daily he waited for news at the village post. As the Poona papers arrived, he devoured their contents. He hastened to explain and discuss the latest news not only with his comrades and schoolmates but even with his schoolmasters and elders. With a view to achieve his objective of driving out the British, Savarkar with friends—Mhaskar, Page and Babarao—formed a Friends' Union called Mitra Mela at the beginning of 1900 (Keer,

1950: 9). Chosen youth were secretly initiated into the fold. This was the famous Beehive of revolutionaries in Western India. "The Mitra Mela grew into the world famous Abhinava Bharat Society in 1904 with a network in Central and Western India and subsequent branches in the form of Ghadar Party resounded in England, France, Burma etc.... Its aim was the political independence of India, to be won by an armed revolt, if need be" (Keer, 1950: 9).

Having finished his school he joined Fergusson College in 1902. His biographers inform us that he was blessed with the gift of thought and speech and was able to impress one and all. It resulted in the formation of a Savarkar group. The group also started a hand-written weekly named *Aryan Weekly*. The weekly mentioned articles on patriotism, literature, history, and science written by Savarkar. One of those brilliant articles was *Saptapadi* in which he dealt with the seven stages of evolution that have to be thought about by a subject nation. He also read Indian and Western classics and learnt the flowery style of writing. He had studied Kalidas and Bhavabhuti also. Shakespeare and Milton were among the English poets who influenced him greatly. Moreover, his biographers tell us he often gave scholarly talks on the revolutions in Italy, Netherlands and America.

In 1902, Savarakar wrote one essay for the magazine *Kaal*. The essay concluded with a powerful vision. "Hindus are responsible for the poverty and disorganization of Hindustan. But if they ever desire to attain prosperity, they must remain Hindus" (Keer, 1950: 22). This bold characteristic of his nationalism distinguished him from other nationalists like Tilak. In 1903, at the opening of the new session of the college, he amidst deafening applause gave a talk on India's glorious past and lamented her loss of freedom. His speech infused courage into the craven-hearted and fired them all with the spirit of patriotism.

Savarkar was an excellent student of history and contemporary events. His interpretation of the political circumstances reveals his desire to create a distinct form of nationalism and patriotism. As Keer notes, "A change in political tone was coming on with the growing tension; a new spirit of self-reliance began to gain ground. Tilak played a role in this. At the same time, Lala Lajpat Rai, Surendranath Banerjee and Gokhale encouraged people with their words. The Swadeshi Movement too was gaining ground. Opposition to the partition of Bengal was coming to a head in October 1905; Hindus opposed it while Muslims supported it. Tilak had made the partition of Bengal an All India issue. Savarkar resolved to unfurl the banner of boycott of foreign goods and urged his countrymen to stop buying everything that was English" (Keer, 1950: 28).

Meanwhile, as we are informed by his biographers, Savarkar was awarded a scholarship to study law in London by PanditShyamji Krishna Varma, then resident of London. He left Mumbai for London on June 9, 1906.[2] After reaching London, he stayed at the India House founded by Pandit Shyamji K. Varma. In due course he was admitted to the prestigious Cray's Inn.

II

It was, in fact, at India House where Savarkar found his mentor and later came into his own. Shyamji Krishna Varma founded India House in 1905 when he purchased the extensive building located at 65 Cromwell Avenue in London's Highgate neighborhood. Krishna Varma, a well-known revolutionary in his own right, served as a guide for the young Vinayak. He also introduced him to the wide circle of like-minded Indian students living in England. As far as his political approach was concerned, he himself repudiated violence and took a non-combative tone with the British public. He often wrote letters to London newspapers in favour of India and used the arguments of British and Western thinkers as support. In the first two years of its existence, India House, under the stewardship of Krishna Varma, was not the bastion of extremism as it became later on. In its time, it served largely as a boarding house and community centre for Indian students arriving in London for study. Many students in these first few years noted that the political nature of India House was not unanimously against British rule and that Krishna Varma teachings were often quite soft. Later on, as we will see, India House began to represent the centre of the radical Indian student movement in Great Britain. It became an organization that not only spoke about an independent India, but was even willing to take up arms for the cause.

In 1905, Krishna Varma had also founded the Indian Home Rule Society. It was a group whose aim was Home Rule as the name suggests. Savarkar soon became part of it. Krishna Varma also started the publication of an English monthly newspaper, *The Indian Sociologist.* It was an intellectual platform to discuss political, religious, and social issues. It was declared as 'An organ of Freedom and of Political, Social and Religious Reform' (Sampath, 2019: 121). It was only 'mild in its criticism of British rule' which focused on how 'India and England should severe their connection peacefully and part as friends' (Sampath, 2019: 121). *The Indian Sociologists* was written in English and its first issue came out in January, 1905. It was aimed at a British audience and intended to function as a 'genuine Indian interpreter' in the UK. The first issue mentioned, "The political relations between England and India urgently require a genuine Indian interpreter in the United Kingdom to show, on behalf of India, how Indians really fare and feel under British rule. No systematic attempt has, so far as our knowledge goes, ever been made in this country by Indians themselves to enlighten the British public with regard to the grievances, demands and aspirations of the people of India and its unrepresented millions before the bar of public opinion in Great Britain and Ireland" (qtd. in Schaffel, 2012: 28).

Indian Sociologist was widely read in Great Britain, India, and even the United States. It was in circulation even after the British tried to prohibit its import from 1907 onward. Krishna Varma presented his views and beliefs about Indian independence in this journal. On the tone of Krishna Varma, Schaffel notes, 'His position was not only the righteous one, but also supported by unsentimental, British logic' (*ibid.*, 28). Interestingly, Krishna Varma placed two quotations from Herbert Spencer at the top of every issue of *Indian Sociologist*. These were, "Every man is free to do that which he wills, provided he infringes not the equal freedom of any other man," and "Resistance to aggression is not simply justifiable but imperative. Non-resistance hurts both altruism and egoism" (*ibid.*, 28). Krishna Varma believed that these, simple but affecting, statements encapsulated the essential aspects of the anti-imperial movement. He also thought that they also explained both the injustice of British rule and the justice of Indian resistance.

Despite making a very impressive effort, the *Indian Sociologist* was not very radical. The contents of the paper were also not very aggressive. Articles were mostly simple commentaries on events or individuals that engaged in Indian affairs in London. It also published commentaries on international affairs that were similarly struggling for independence.

However, the nature of India House drastically changed after the arrival of Savarkar. The goal for India House remained the same as Krishna Varma set its ultimate ends, but after the arrival of Savarkar India House took a decidedly distinct turn. The first change was Savarkar's creation of the Free India Society in 1906. It, in fact, replaced the India Home Rule Society.[3] The name of Savarkar's organization symbolizes one of the major differences between Savarkar's and Krishna Varma's philosophies. Savarkar's philosophy and activism was to 'free India' from the oppression of British rule. This was a more radical stance than Krishna Varma who thought like many moderate leaders of his time only about Indian Home Rule. Savarkar, in this sense was far ahead of his other counterparts. Like many other nationalists, he used to spread his revolutionary ideas through pamphlets, booklets and books.[4] These materials show the nature of the future of the struggle for independence for India. By naming his group the Free India Society, he made it entirely clear that Indian and British interests were diametrically opposed. It also shows the nature of Savarkar's mode of politics. As Jyotirmaya Sharma explains, "Savarkar's politics was one that divided the world between 'friend' and 'foe'. It was not material who the 'foe' was as long as an enemy could be found at all times" (Sharma, 2007: 17-18). Later in his career, Savarkar would identify this foe as Muslim, but during his time in London, the British represented the central evil for the Indians.

Savarkar also rejected the practice set by Krishna Varma that focused on cordiality with the British Press. He made it clear that he had no intention of extending this cordiality. He chose to write only letters in Marathi to be published in local Indian newspapers. Further, India House which had an inclusive atmosphere during Krishna Varma's time, disappeared with Savarkar's rise. Schaffel notes a case in this regard. He notes the case of David Garnett, a young Irish revolutionary living in London during the period, who visited India House during the summer of 1909, and mentioned the distinctively non-British environment cultivated by Savarkar, "There is one important incident that might be pointed out to Savarkar's nationalistic politics. As seen with Krishna Varma's decision to open India House with a British speaker, India House had often included the British on even its most important occasions. Where the India Home Rule Society had been modelled after a Victorian public association, with the goal of parting from the British 'as friends', there now stood the Free India Society promising to 'engage in a bloody and relentless war' against the foreigner" (qtd. in Schaffel, 2012: 34).

All the biographers note that Savarkar saw the Free India Society and India House as extensions of the *Abhinav Bharat* that he had left behind in Maharashtra. Nevertheless, Savarkar knew that the real struggle for Indian independence had to be fought in India, not on foreign soil or in London. But the location of India House was very useful for him as it allowed him some short of liberty that was not possible in India. It is also pertinent to note that Krishna Varma had maintained a minimum relationship with India. This had further limited the amount of interaction between India House and Indian revolutionary groups in India. On the other hand, all biographers note, Savarkar not only maintained his connections with local *Abhinav Bharat* leaders throughout India but also treated India House as a training ground to prepare members for the battles.

In London, Savarkar received both practical and philosophical training. He took significant advantage of the freedoms offered by British officials. These officials, although somewhat concerned about activities at India House, were initially unwilling to actively interfere in the group's pursuits. "While members of the Free India Society were taught how to make bombs, shoot firearms, and were often called upon to smuggle weapons into India on their return trips home" (Schaffel, 2012: 35). Schaffel further notes that "a Russian bomb-making manual that had made its way to India House *via* Paris was copied and given to India House members with instructions to pass the information on to at least one hundred other Indians once they made it back to India" (*ibid.*, p.35). It shows his revolutionary politics and mode of working from the perspective of "we *versus* them".

Certain events inform us about Savarkar's mode of thought and working in London. They affirm his nationalism and patriotism. In the summer of 1907, in order to mark the anniversary of the Sepoy Mutiny, Savarkar designed small medallions with the words "In Memory of the Martyrs of 1857" and "Bande Mataram". They were worn by Indian students in support of the nationalist cause. As one of the biographers notes,

> "In 1907 the English people took it into their head to celebrate the 50th Anniversary of their victory over the mutineers of 1857. Dramas and lectures and special numbers of daily leading papers in India and in England vied with each other to revive the memory of 1857 and revile the so-called mutineers in the most scurrilous manner that hatred could conceive. To counteract this vilifying campaign and relate the story of the national rising faithfully and truly Mr. Savarkar organized a counter campaign to honour the memory of Indian leaders of 1857—Nana Saheb, the Queen of Zansi, Tatya Tope, Kumar Sing, Maulavi Ahmed Saheb and the rest. It was so bold a step to take, in the very heart of the British capital to honour Nana Saheb and Tatya Tope whom the common run of Englishmen thought some species of demoniacal order that almost all noted Indian leaders instinctively shrank from it. But Mr. Savarkar had the youth by him. A great and memorable meeting was held at India House, fasts were observed, a vow to undergo a week of self-denial was taken, pamphlets named "Oh Martyrs" were distributed in thousands in England and India, students

> boldly appeared in Oxford and Cambridge and the Inns of Court wearing beautifully carved badges of "Honours to the Martyrs of 1857" on their breasts. In streets and trains individual scuffle ensued. Even in a college, the English professors lost their temper and ejaculated at the sight of the badge borne by the Indian students "Martyrs? They were murderers! Remove the badge." There upon the Indian students demanded an apology from the said professors for insulting their national heroes and as a protest left the College in a body. Some lost their scholarships, same voluntarily resigned it; some were recalled by their partners. The political atmosphere in England grew daily more and more electrical. The Indian Government began to feel restless" (Chitragupta, 1986: 77).

Another significant event related to Savarkar in London is the celebration of the birth anniversary of Guru Gobind Singh on 29th December, 1909. The Life informs, 'A grand festival was organized and a ceremonious meeting held in London, to celebrate the birthday of Guru Gobind Singh. Lala Lajpatrai, Bepin Chandra Pal and several other prominent Hindus paid glowing tributes to the memory of the 'hero'. In one of his eloquent speeches, Savarkar referred to him as "the prophet, the warrior, the poet". The most spirited pamphlet that he wrote especially for that occasion was named 'Khalsa' and which, despite proscription orders found its way to schools and colleges in Punjab. Savarkar also wrote a book in Marathi on the History of Sikhs—but unfortunately it was swallowed by the 'Postal Box' and 'never could be traced back'.

The composition and nature of India House during Savarkar's time signal a fascinating issue. This is very much relevant to the origin and development of Savarkar's Hindutva, (Schaffel, 2015: 38). Schaffel notes that India House and the Free India Society were overwhelmingly Hindu. Although Savarkar occasionally cited Mazzini, he more often turned to Hindu scriptures such as the *Ramayana*, *Mahabharat* and *Bhagavad Gita*. Savarkar argued that the text justified violence against those who would harm Mother India.

An interesting case of Gandhi-Savarkar debate on the occasion of Vijayadashmi is worth mentioning here. Gandhi met Savarkar , second time, on 24 October 1909. The Indian community gathered to celebrate the festival of Vijayadashmi. Nearly seventy Indians took part. Gandhi was invited to preside over the meeting. He agreed on the condition that 'no controversial politics were to be touched upon'. He also told, he would rather speak about the greatness of the *Ramayana*. He spoke,

> "Everyone, whether Hindu, Muslim or Parsi, should be proud of belonging to a country, which produced a man like Shri Ramachandra. To the extent that he was a great Indian, he should be honoured by every Indian. For the Hindus, he is a god. If India again produced a Ramachandra, a Sita, a Lakshmana and a Bharata, she would attain prosperity in no time. It should be remembered, of course, that before Ramachandra qualified for public service, he suffered exile in the forest for 12 years. Sita went through extreme suffering and Lakshmana lived without sleep all those years and observed celibacy. When Indians learn to live in that manner, they can, from that instant count themselves as free men. India has no other way of achieving happiness for herself" (qtd. in Sampath, 2019: 225).

As Sampath notes, "It was then Vinayak's turn to speak. Indirectly puncturing holes in Gandhi's arguments, he said that it would be worthwhile to remember that Vijayadashmi is preceded by a nine-day fast to propitiate Goddess Durga, who is a symbol of war and annihilation of evil. He concurred with Gandhi that Ramachandra was the life and soul of India but urged the audience to remember that even he could not establish Rama Rajya (his kingdom) without slaying Ravana who symbolized tyranny, aggression and injustice. If Ramachandra had merely sat on a fast, it was unlikely that his kingdom could have been established. He went on: Hindus are the heart of Hindustan. Nevertheless, just as the beauty of the rainbow is not impaired but enhanced by its varied hues, so also Hindustan will look all the more beautiful across the sky of future by assimilating all the best from the Muslim, Parsee, Jewish and other civilizations" (Sampath, 2019: 225-26). It demonstrates how Savarkar conceived of Hinduism and how his approach differed greatly from Gandhi's Hinduism.

Although Savarkar's upbringing in a spiritually pious family had a heavy influence on him; yet his interpretation of Hinduism was quite different. During his London days, he developed a particular Hindu identity and especially his reliance on Hindu religious texts as justification for his ideological beliefs, eventually separated many non-Hindus wishing to join his cause. Certainly, as noted by one of the scholars, "there is no proof that Savarkar and the members of India House were intentionally excluding Muslims or Christians from joining, but it seems likely that an environment of almost exclusively Hindu tenour would have imbued Savarkar with the roots of an ardent loyalty to his fellow Hindus" (Julia, 2015: 56).

As we consider the roots of Savarkar's Hindutva, it is imperative to examine some of the other influences on him. These influences are often manifested during his early life, especially in London.[5] As mentioned before, Savarkar was a strong admirer of Mazzini. Mazzini was the Italian revolutionary who worked to form a united Italian Republic in opposition to the occupation by the Austrian Empire.[6] When Savarkar arrived in London, his first significant act was to publish a Marathi translation of Mazzini's biography.[7] It shows how the Italian revolution shaped the thinking process of Savarkar. Although Savarkar quoted Mazzini less in his writings and speech, Mazzini's influence on him cannot be undermined. The reason for influence may be that both thought independence from foreign rule could only be achieved through a unification of the populace against occupying power. Also, at that time, both India and Italy were quite fragmented and many smaller states had a great deal of autonomy within the nation. In order to effectively oppose foreign rule, it was essential to unite these divergent states under one banner.In addition, Mazzini and Savarkar both held the view that a popular uprising is the required method to unify the nation and it is only through it that one can throw out external power. Both also advocated for a violent revolution to continue until such an end was achieved.

All biographers note that Savarkar was highly influenced by Shivaji since his childhood. Shivaji was a seventeenth-century Indian king who founded the Maratha kingdom in India. By the late nineteenth century, he was projected as a Hindu patriot who resisted Mughal dominance. According to the traditional story of his life, at the age twenty-five he began gathering followers and attacking Mughal outposts and strongholds, amassing a large army along the way. His story and history both indicate that he failed in his mission to free India from the Mughals. Yet he succeeded in establishing and managing an independent Hindu kingdom that he ruled till his lifetime. Shivaji symbolizes a reviver of Hindu spirit and religion during a period which was heavily overshadowed by Muslim rule.[8] Shivaji, importantly, remained the symbol and icon of Hindu nationalism even before Savarkar. In this regard most prominent was Bal Gangadhar Tilak who was also influenced by Shivaji.

Two prominent intellectual figures, Johann Kaspar Bluntschli and Herbert Spencer, influenced and shaped Savarkar's notion of Hindutva. Both these thinkers were political theorists and their views on the evolution of society and the state undoubtedly influenced the development of Savarkar's own ideology.

Bluntschli was a Swiss jurist who most famously wrote *The Theory of the Modern State* (1885). In his work he compared states to organic bodies. He argued that, like an organic body, the state had a similar cycle of life, growth, and death. Bluntschli believed strongly in national unification—specifically, in the cases of Germany and Italy. He suggested that many of the smaller, individual states within these policies would not be capable of surviving on their own. This appealed directly to Savarkar. He also saw his own country as fragmented and in need of national unification. It is only through the strength of a united India that it could get rid of the British yoke. Bluntschli's influence on Savarkar may be substantiated by the fact, as he noted in prison memoir *My Transportation for Life,* that Bluntschli's *Theory of the Modern State* was included in the prison library which he assembled in the Cellular Jail. It suggests the importance of Bluntschli's work to him.

Savarkar was highly influenced by Spencer also. He first read Spencer in Nasik. Sampath notes, "His young mind struggled to gather the complete purport of Herbert Spencer's *Liberal Utilitarianism.* Many years later in England, when he asked people who had read Spencer in English, he realized to his amazement that the Marathi translations of Spencer's works that he had studied in Nashik had given him more knowledge than those who read the originals" (Sampath, 2019: 88).

Herbert Spencer, like Bluntschli, equated states with living bodies. He developed a term the 'social organism' to describe society within his theoretical system. His ideas made an impact on political theory also. Spencer emphasized individualism and it was perhaps the most integral part of all of his theory. It also included the notion of 'survival of the fittest' and saw evolution leading towards some ideal.

It is worth remembering here that Krishna Varma's *Indian Sociologist* regularly quoted Spencer on its front page. Certainly Spencer's beliefs and logic were appealing to Savarkar. Spencer's vehement disapproval of imperialism also undoubtedly added to Savarkar's admiration of him. But Savarkar gave a twist to Spencer's theory and justified his own belief in the preeminence of Hindu rights over those of minority groups. As Julia Swift notes, "Indeed, by combining Spencer's ideas about the inevitable evolution of the state towards some broader goal, and the concept of "survival of the fittest," it is easy to see how Savarkar – who indubitably saw Hindus as "the fittest" —may have justified to himself a vision of a future Hindu nation, superior to all others" (Julia, 2015: 63).

Having seen the intellectual formation of Savarkar in London, now consider the key London events to comprehend his politics till his arrest and extradition to India in 1910. As noted, Savarkar took over the leadership of India House and the Free India Society after Krishna Varma's departure from London in 1907. Savarkar, as his biographers note, promoted his goals of training Indian revolutionaries for targeted acts of violence towards the British. They also smuggled weapons and books back to India. The most dramatic event during his stay in London was the killing of William Curzon-Wyllie by Madan Lal Dhingra on July 1, 1909. Dhingra was an Indian student living in London who attended Savarkar's lectures. It was found by the police that Savarkar was a primary conspirator in the assassination. As Schaffel notes in his analysis of the event, Dhingra may have seemed a strange choice of hit man, but "[his] absence at most India House events represents not his lack of interest in India House's radical message, but rather his own beliefs that the speakers and meetings were 'mere talk' and not worth attending" (Schaffel, 2012: 82).

Dhingra was the ideal student that Savarkar had been searching for since his rise to the leadership of India House. Dhingra explained the reasoning behind his willingness to sacrifice himself in his last statement before his hanging: "The only lesson required in India at present is to learn how to die and the only way to teach it is by dying ourselves. Therefore I die and glory in my martyrdom! This war of independence will continue between India and England, so long as the Hindu and the English races last" (Schaffel, 2012: 83).

Savarkar led India House till the summer of 1909. In addition to 'theoretical' and 'practical' lessons, he provided the Free India Society with what was considered essential for the bloody resistance against the British. He also provided support to his compatriots in India. In summer 1909 he moved to Paris. There were several reasons for moving to Paris. "Given the massive outrage and hostility in London against Indian students in general, and him in particular, and because of his precarious health, Vinayak decided to move to Paris. Shyamji and Madame Cama had been prevailing upon him for a long time to relocate to Paris" (Sampath, 2019: 110).

III

Having discussed Savarkar's London days, his ideological affiliation that shaped his notion of Hindutva, now discuss the political events in India that sharpened his formulations of Hindutva. One well argue that it was the political materiality of India that might have influenced his notion of Hindutva. In Indian politics, the time period of 1905-1910 was not only about the moderate-extremist debate. One may remind that throughout 1907 and 1908, heated debates were also held regarding 'separate electorates'. It was the matter of the 'weightage' proposed by the Muslim deputation and subsequently consented to by Viceroy Lord Minto. The Muslim leadership showed their apprehension that the Hindu majority would not be able to deal with Muslims suitably and fairly. They also argued that Hindus and Muslims had vast social, cultural, and religious differences. They also pointed out that Muslims should get a more significant representation in the different councils. They gave a strange logic for it. The deputation stated that Muslims had ruled India for 700 years before the British arrival. Thus they had a natural claim to additional political importance, which must be reflected in the councils. They also stated that the community had played a vital role in defending the country. As history informs us the Morley-Minto Reforms of 1909 awarded separate Muslim electorates for Muslims. In this reform, the number of Muslim members in the council was much more than the numerical strength of their population. This may be seen as the seed of two separate nations that manifested later on. Savarkar as a good reader of political events must have sensed the meaning and implications of that reform.

We note Savarkar's direct intervention in Indian politics in the case of the Mopla rebellion. The Mopla rebellion occurred from August 20, 1921 to 1922 in the Malabar region of Kerala. It began as a revolt against British colonial rule. The uprising was also against the prevailing feudal system controlled by elite Hindus. The British had appointed high caste Hindus in positions of authority to get their support. As a result, the protest turned against Hindus. At the time, the Indian National Congress repudiated the movement and it remained isolated from the wider national movement.[9]

Sampath notes Savarkar strongly 'condemned the barbarity of the Moplahs' and the 'pusillanimity with which the Congress reacted' to this, just to save their movement. Savarkar also wrote several essays and articles warning people about the dangers and realities of the Khilafat and pan-Islamism movement—many of which were published after his release from jail. He wondered why there was no open debate or discussion with the Hindus of the country on whether they wanted to align with such a movement. Sampath notes, Savarkar "lamented that most Hindus were not even aware of the history of political Islam or its theology. No wonder some of them had made generous invitations to the Khalifa to shift to India where he would be crowned as the unofficial religious-political head of all Indian Muslims. What kind of a suicidal and ignorant step was this? Vinayak questioned" (Sampath, 2019: 468).

Savarkar responded to the baffling question of his time. He attempted to give an intellectual response to the fundamental question of Hindu identity and unification. This was despite his difficult conditions of prison life and his failing health. The response was in English which shows his intention was beyond the Marathi-speaking people. It was targeted at the country at large. In place of mentioning his own name as author of his work, he mentioned 'A Maratha'. The work was smuggled out of prison and later published by Narayan Rao. Sampath notes, "Right from his childhood, Vinayak had bemoaned the lack of unity and organization in Hindu society, ridden as it was with innumerable caste differences and other complexities. Finding an answer to 'Who is a Hindu?' seemed germane to him at this point of time. From the confines of jail, he had been watching with alarm Gandhi taking the Hindu community for a ride during the Khilafat agitation. The relative increase in the Muslim population that the census had established, and the uncertain status of untouchables and tribal groups as Hindus for enumeration purposes made the definition of a Hindu all the more critical (*ibid.*, 470). Savarkar took help of history to create a sense of Hindu identity, pride and belonging in his book *Hindutva*. Recall, Hindu identity has been an ongoing nationalistic project for a long time. "As Right from the ancient saints such as Adi Shankara, Ramanuja, Madhwa, to the medieval Bhakti and Sufi poets, to modern reformers such as Dayanand Saraswati, Ramakrishna Paramahamsa, Vivekananda, Tilak, Aurobindo Ghose, and even Mahatma Gandhi—there has always been a call for revival of what was known as Indian values and cultural identity" (*ibid.*, 471). However, it was Savarkar who extended the word 'Hindutva' beyond religious adherence. He gave a new meaning to Hindutva in terms of ethnic nationalism.[10]

The style, form and content of his text *Hindutva* shows his intellectual power and influence. In his booklet *Hindutva*, he emphasized 'Hindu unity', equating it with Indian culture with the values of 'Hindu civilization'. He also portrayed the vision of a Hindu Rashtra that belonged only to those who treated India as their 'Fatherland' and 'Holyland'.

NOTES

1. *Life of Barrister Savarkar* was first published in 1926 with a pen name Chitragupta. There have been various allusions about who is the author of this biography. It ranges from Congress leader C. Rajagopalachari, the revolutionary V.V.S. Aiyar to Savarkar himself writing under a pseudonym. The identity of the author continues to remain a mystery. The second edition of this biography was published in 1987 by Veer Savarkar Prakashan Bombay. Dr. Ravindra Vaman Das wrote the preface to this book on 26 February, 1986. In this study, the author has used the second edition, in

the form of the e-book, of this biography downloaded from https://savarkar.org/en/pdfs/life_of_barrister_savarkar_by_chitragupta.pdf. Dhananajay Keer biography *Savarkar and his Times* was first published in 1950 by A.V. Keer, Bombay. It has been pointed out by many critics that Keer's biography is more of a hagiography than a biography. In this study, I have used his biography in a very limited way. Further, I have used the first edition of his biography. Vikram Sampath (2019) in his biography *Savarkar: Echoes From a Forgotten Past*, attempts to document the life events of Savarkar between 1883 and 1924. The book provides a detailed description of Savarkar's early childhood days, his life as a law student in London and his activities in London in full detail. This chapter uses an e-book of the above title downloaded from https://dokumen.pub/download/savarkar-echoes-from-a-forgotten-past-.html on 10 March 2021. Here we will focus on these three books and other related materials to examine the root and development of his philosophy of Hindutva.

2. It is worth mentioning that the year 1906 was a landmark in Indian politics. It is the year when Savarkar travelled to London; saw the birth of the Muslim League at Dacca. During those days revolutionaries from the world over took shelter in London. Savarkar sought to learn how to organize a revolution and carry on the struggle for freedom by inculcating this spirit in the bright Indian students there.
3. We are also informed by the biographers that he began to organize Indian students like Bhai Parmananda, Lala Hardayal, Virendranath Chattopadhyaya (brother of Sarojini Naidu), V.V.S. Aiyar, Gyanchand Varma, Madame Cama, Senapati Bapat etc. in London.
4. He devoted his time and energy to foreign propaganda. He was the first and foremost Indian leader who perceived and foresaw the impact of vital forces in international politics. He wrote articles on Indian affairs and got them translated into French, Russian, German, Italian etc. to acquaint the civilized world with Indian affairs and enlist their support for the cause of Indian freedom. With these objectives in mind, he had deputed Madame Cama to the International Socialists Congress in Germany in 1907, where, in spite of British opposition the Conference moved but did not pass a resolution on India and unfurled the flag of independence of India which was designed by Savarakar. The delegates rose and saluted the flag. ... An admirer of the Sikhs, he learnt Gurumukhi, read the Adi Granth, Panth-Surya Prakash etc., and issued many pamphlets, called Khalsa. Issued in Gurumukhi, these made the Sikh soldiers conscious of their duty.
5. It is significant to note that Savarkar was a highly intellectual person. He read both eastern and western classics. Sampath notes, "Vinayak had made an in-depth study of all the dramas of Kalidasa and Bhavabhuti, the legendary playwrights of Sanskrit literature. In an essay, he brilliantly contrasted their styles. The English poets Scott, Shakespeare and Milton influenced him the most. Milton's *Paradise Lost* was among his favourite works and he had even learnt many of its cantos by heart. His extensive reading found

its reflection in his insightful writings. His essay 'Ramayana and Iliad' that compares the two most famous epics was a masterpiece that won him much acclaim even from his professors. Jeremy Bentham, John Stuart Mill and Herbert Spencer's political philosophy made a lasting impact on him. Vinayak was particularly impressed by the utilitarian philosophy of Bentham and Mill. He writes, 'In college days I read Bentham and Mill and . . . based my moral thinking on the lines of utilitarian principles as explained by them... Not only that, I would teach this utilitarian philosophy even in our revolutionary organizations'. While he wrote plays later in his life, as a student of Fergusson College, he even acted in two of them—a minor role in the play titled *Tratika* in 1902 and the role of Iago in *Zunzarrao*, the Marathi version of *Othello*, in 1904 (Sampath, 2019: 136).

6. Giuseppe Mazzini (1805-1872) was exiled to France at the age of twenty-six after joining a revolutionary group that plotted to overthrow the absolutist Italian government. While living in Marseille, he founded the famous Young Italy, a group created to unify the divided Italian states and throw off the yoke of foreign rule. A staunch republican, Mazzini believed strongly in a democratically governed Italy. However, although Italy did achieve unification during his lifetime, it was ruled by a monarchy – a major disappointment for him. He died after years of discouraging setbacks and defeats, forced to face the failure of his vision for an Italian Republic. After his death, Mazzini remained a relatively controversial figure, with some celebrating him as a hero and others claiming that he betrayed his country. In many ways, therefore, the lives of Mazzini and Savarkar can be seen as parallel to each other. It is no wonder that the young Indian was so drawn to the ideas put forth by his Italian predecessor.
7. Chitragupta notes, "No sooner he reached London he began the translation of Mazzini's writings into Marathi and within a year of his departure from India had it finished to secure a record sale in Marathi literature. All leading newspapers reviewed "Savarkar's Mazzini" in leading articles. Students were made by their teachers, and sons by their fathers, to commit whole passages to memories from the masterly introduction which Mr. Savarkar wrote for the book. In some places the volume was taken out with religious books in procession, and when years after it secured the last distinction which is the general fate of such books and was proscribed by the Government hunted out and destroyed" (Chitragupta, 1987: 76).
8. Significantly, as author James Laine discusses in his historiographic analysis, *Shivaji: Hindu King in Islamic India*, a great deal of the commonly accepted knowledge about Shivaji is actually myth and legend that has emerged in the centuries since his death. What has become apparent is that the truth surrounding specific details of this Maharashtrian hero is far less significant than the ideals that he represents (see Sampath, 2019: 169).
9. "The Muslim League too justified the Moplah outrage as a religious war against the British, in which the Hindus got caught in the crossfire as they were seen to be aiding the colonial masters. The Khilafat conference in its

session at Cocanada held in 1923 expressed its solidarity with the Moplah 'martyrs'. Shaukat Ali moved a resolution calling it a duty of every Muslim towards the brave Moplahs to provide for the maintenance of one Moplah orphan. He and his brother would take the initiative for this. This was after the government intervened and crushed the uprising with a heavy hand, leaving several Moplahs dead" (Sampath, 2019: 468).

10. About the constant insinuations about the book being anode of hatred, especially towards the Muslims, historian Janaki Bakhle opines: Savarkar is widely reviled in Indian history as an apostle of hate; through a reading of Hindutva I argue that he might better be understood as a spurned lover... Hindutva in its time was also a reminder to a Hindu community that even if Gandhi had left the political milieu, there was no need to worry. A political Hindu and a true nationalist was back and ready to lead India, even from behind prison walls. Hindutva was a pugilistic punch thrown against Gandhi in the competitive political ring for national leadership. Elucidating the importance of this book, she further writes that *Hindutva* is one of the few texts written by an Indian nationalist that links the present Hindu moment of Indian history to the pre-independence anticolonial period.

REFERENCES

Chitragupta. (1987). *Life of Barrister Savarkar*. Bombay: Veer Savarkar Prakashan. https://savarkar.org/en/pdfs/life_of_barrister_savarkar_by_chitragupta.pdf.

Julia, Kelley-Swift. (2015). *A Misunderstood Legacy: V.D. Savarkar and the Creation of Hindutva.* A thesis submitted to the faculty of Wesleyan University. Middletown, Connecticut. http://citeseerx.ist.psu.edu/viewdoc/download pdf. Downloaded on 26 June, 2020.

Jyotirmaya Sharma. (2007). "History as Revenge and Retaliation: Rereading Savarkar's 'the War of Independence of 1857'," *Economic and Political Weekly* 42, No. 19: 1718.

Keer, Dhananjay. (1950). *Savarkar and His Times.* Bombay: A.V. Keer.

Paul Schaffel. (2012). "Empire and Assassination: Indian Students, 'India House', and Information Gathering in Great Britain, 1898-1911" (Wesleyan University, 2012). http://www.pwsfoundation.org/pdfs/PWS_Schaffel_ Paul_ 2012_Thesis.pdf .

Sampath, Vikram. (2019). *Savarkar Echoes from a Forgotten Past 1883-1924.* India : Penguin.

4

Gandhi and *The Essence of Hinduism*

"Let us reproduce in ourselves the true Hindu spirit, and then ask whether it satisfies the soul or not"

(CWMG 35: 525)

We discussed the origin and development of Gandhi's notion of Hinduism in the first chapter based on his writings. Throughout this chapter, we will explore his views on the central characteristics and the philosophical basis of Hinduism. We will again refer to Gandhi's original writings for this. Gandhi did not write a systematic book on Hinduism, as Ambedkar and Savarkar wrote, but his scattered views on Hindu religion can be categorized and analyzed to get his comprehensive picture of the Hindu religion.[1] I hope that this will be helpful in understanding Gandhi's philosophy of Hinduism more specifically. The chapter is divided into four parts. The first part focuses on Gandhi's definition of Hindu, Hinduism and its chief characteristics. The second part deals with the division which Gandhi makes between historical Hinduism and philosophical Hinduism. The third part focuses on the problems within Hinduism and Gandhi's interpretation and response to them. The fourth part deals with the philosophical structure of Gandhi's Hinduism.

I

Gandhi was often asked, "Who is a Hindu?" He was also asked several times as to what is the 'origin' of the word Hindu and is 'there any Hinduism?' Gandhi replied to these questions in one of his prayer speeches and they were reported in his journal *Harijan* published on 30.11.1947. The report mentions that Gandhi was no historian, but he had read in some authentic book on Hinduism that the word 'Hindu' did not occur in the Vedas. On the origin of the term Hindu, Gandhi held the view that when Alexander the Great invaded India, the inhabitants of the country to the East of the Sindhu, which is known by the English-speaking Indians as the Indus, were described as Hindus. Later on, the letter 'S' had become 'H' in Greek. Thus the religion of these inhabitants became Hinduism. Gandhi also informs us that it also gave shelter to the early Christians who had fled from persecution, also to the Jews known as Beni-Israil and also to the Parsis. The report in *Harijan* further notes, 'Aryan scholars swore by what they called Vedic religion and Hindustan was otherwise known as Aryavarta' (Gandhi, 1996: 1). Thus, Gandhi, on the naming of Hindu, accepts the geographical argument that the word Hindu signifies a religion professed by the inhabitants of the country to the East of Sindhu. Gandhi mentions several qualifications for being a Hindu aside from this name. Defining who is Hindu, as early as 1926, he mentioned "In a concrete manner he is a Hindu who believes in God, immortality of the soul, transmigration, the law of *Karma* and *Moksha*, and who tries to practice Truth and *Ahimsa* in daily life, and therefore, practices cow-protection in its widest sense and understands and tries to act according to the law of Varnashrama" (*ibid*., 3). Thus, Gandhi accepts not only geographical argument but moves beyond it and views Hindu from quite a different perspective.

He also brings the argument of heredity into his definition of who is Hindu. He once tried to define the question of why he is Hindu. He replies that 'believing as I do in the influence of heredity, being born in a Hindu family, I have remained a Hindu' (*ibid*., 27). The most interesting aspect of his discussion about Hindu is that he called himself 'Sanatani Hindu'. He noted that 'the word 'Sanatana' he used is in its 'natural sense'. He admitted, "I call myself a Sanatani Hindu, because, (1) I believe in the Vedas, the Upanishads, the Puranas and all that goes by the name of Hindu scriptures, and therefore, in *avatars* and rebirth, (2) I believe in the *varnashrama dharma* in a sense in my opinion strictly Vedic but not in its present popular and crude sense, (3) I believe in the protection of the cow in its much larger sense than the popular, (4) I do not disbelieve in idol-worship" (*ibid*., 31). In another writing he made his definition more explicit with some clarification, "I call myself Sanatani Hindu, because I believe in the Vedas, Upanishads, the Puranas and the writings left by the holy reformers. This belief does not require me to accept as authentic everything that passes as *Shastras*. I reject everything that contradicts the fundamental principles of morality. I am not required to accept the *ipse dixit* or the interpretations of *pandits*. Above all I call myself a Sanatani Hindu, so long as the Hindu society in general accepts me as such" (*ibid*., 3).

Gandhi also attempted to define what is Hinduism? He mentioned that "If I were asked to define the Hindu creed I should simply say: search after Truth through non-violent means. A man may not believe even in God and still he may call himself a Hindu" (*ibid.*, 3).

A reader confronted his definition of Hindu, especially the latter part of it, and asked a question as to whether a person who denies God can be called Hindu (*ibid.*, 4). Gandhi replied, "Denial of the existence of God is not a characteristic of Hinduism. Millions of Hindus do believe in God. Therefore, one may say 'there are Hindus who believe in God, etc.' But 'a man may not believe in God and still call himself a Hindu'. In the second case I have attempted an exhaustive definition. In the first case, I have given a fairly general illustration. I, therefore, see no conflict between the two positions" (*ibid.*, 4).

Gandhi's writings also point out the 'outstanding features of Hinduism'. He noted that non-violence is common to all religions, but it has found the 'highest expression and application in Hinduism' (*ibid.*, 28). It is imperative to mention that Gandhi did not regard Jainism or Buddhism as separate from Hinduism. The most striking feature of Hinduism, according to him, is its belief 'in the oneness not of merely all human life but in the oneness of all that lives' (*ibid.*, 28). Further, in his opinion worshipping cows is Hinduism's 'unique contribution to the evolution of humanitarianism'. As it shows "practical application of the belief in the oneness and, therefore, sacredness, of all life" (*ibid*, 28). In his view, "the profound belief in the 'transmigration' of Hinduism is a direct consequence of this belief." Gandhi also notes that 'the discovery of the law of varnashrama' is also the significant contribution of Hinduism and it is 'a magnificent result of the ceaseless search for truth' (*ibid.*, 28). He noted all these as the "outstanding features of Hinduism" (*ibid.*, 28). Yet it does not mean that he supports cow protection and varnashrama in their present form. He carefully underlines that "the present ideas of cow-worship and varnashrama are a caricature of what in my opinion the originals are" (*ibid.*, 28).

Gandhi also considered Hinduism as the 'tolerant of all religions'. He noted, "On examination I have found it to be the most tolerant of all religions known to me" (*ibid.*, 37). Hinduism is free of dogma, which makes it appealing to him. Further he points out the 'all-embracing' nature of Hinduism (*ibid.*, 37). Glorifying Hinduism he tells us that the 'beauty of Hinduism' lies in its 'all-embracing inclusiveness'. On this ground, he noted that in Hinduism there is room enough for Jesus, as there is for Mohammed, Zoroaster and Moses.[2] Moreover, Hinduism also gives its votaries the 'largest scope for self-expression'. He claims that Hinduism is not an exclusive religion, thus, it enables its followers to 'respect all the other religions'. Moreover, it also enables the followers of Hinduism to 'admire and assimilate whatever may be good in the other faiths' (*ibid.*, 28). 'What is contained in any other religion is always to be found in Hinduism'. His love for Hinduism is so powerful that he goes on to state that 'what is not contained in it is insubstantial or unnecessary' (*ibid.*, 37).

For him, *ahimsa* is 'the chief glory of Hinduism', although it has been sought to be explained in such a way as it is only for Sannyasis. He rejects such views and argues that 'it is the way of life' and India has to 'show it to the world' (*ibid.*, 4). He saw Hinduism as 'a living organism' which is 'liable to growth and decay, and subject to the laws of Nature' (*ibid.*, 5). He claims that 'one and indivisible at the root', Hinduism has grown into a 'vast tree with innumerable branches'. In a very poetic language, he narrates that 'the changes in the seasons affect it'. Thus, 'it has its autumn and summer, its winter and spring'. 'The rains nourish and fructify it too'. Further, for him, Hinduism insists on 'the brotherhood not only of all mankind but of all that lives'. It is a concept that makes one giddy, but we have to work up to it. "The moment we have restored real living equality between man and man, we shall be able to establish equality between man and the whole creation. When that day comes we shall have peace on earth and goodwill to men" (*ibid.*, 5).

For Gandhi, Hinduism implies 'relentless pursuit after truth'. He further observes that it is the good fortune or the misfortune of Hinduism that it has no official creed like other religions. In his view, if today's Hinduism has become moribund, inactive, irresponsive to growth, it is because we are fatigued. He hopes that as soon as the fatigue is over, Hinduism will burst forth upon the world with a brilliance perhaps unknown before.

II

Gandhi is not interested in the history of Hinduism nor its scripture or literary interpretation. He is interested in the 'spirit' of Hinduism. He made a distinction between historical Hinduism and philosophical Hinduism. He wrote, "There are two aspects of Hinduism. There is, on the one hand, the historical Hinduism with its untouchability, superstitious, worship of stocks and stones, animal sacrifice and so on. On the other, we have the Hinduism of the *Gita*, the *Upanishads* and Patanjali's *Yogasutras* which is the acme of *Ahimsa* and oneness of all creation, pure worship of one immanent, formless, imperishable God" (*ibid.*, 4).

This distinction is an insightful clue to understand Gandhi's view on Hinduism. He rejected the historical interpretation of Hindu narratives. This rejection was based on the 'application of the test of Truth and non-violence' to the scriptures. Once a correspondent who criticized his interpretation of Hinduism, Gandhi wrote that he is not a literalist and thus tries to understand the 'spirit' of the various scriptures of the world. He mentioned that he applies the test of Truth and *Ahimsa* laid down by these very scriptures for interpretation., In his words, "I reject what is inconsistent with that test, and I appropriate all that is consistent with it" (*ibid*., 25). For example, he rejected the story of a shudra having been punished by Ramachandra for daring to learn the Vedas as an interpolation. Yet he worshipped Rama because He is the 'perfect being of my conception, not a historical person fact about whose life may vary with the progress of new historical discoveries and researches' (Gandhi, 1994: 10). He also did not consider Tulsidas's *Ramayana* as a work of history and argued that as judged by historical tests, *Ramayana* would be 'fit for the scrap heap'. He argues that Tulsidas had nothing to do with the Rama of history. However 'as a spiritual experience, his book is almost unrivaled at least for me" (*ibid*., 10). Furthermore, he mentions that even as a text based on spiritual experience, he does not rely on every word found in so many editions as the *Ramayana* of Tulsidas. In his words, "It is the spirit running through the book that holds me spellbound" (*ibid*., 10). He also argues that he cannot subscribe to the prohibition against Shudras learning the Vedas—a position Hindus at that time possessed. In fact, in his opinion, 'at the present moment, we are all predominantly shudras, so long as we are serfs'. He clearly mentioned that "Knowledge cannot be the prerogative of any class or section" (*ibid*., 11).

Similarly, Gandhi comments on the Puranas. He identified some stories from the Puranas as being 'most dangerous' in our time. He writes, "The stories told in the Puranas are some of them most dangerous if we do not know their bearing on the present conditions" (*ibid*., 28). Apparently, he believes that details of scripture are not necessarily relevant in our own time, rather they may work as 'death traps'. "The shastras would be death-traps if we were to regulate our conduct according to every detail given in them or according to that of the characters therein described" (*ibid*., 28). For him, shastra are helpful only to the extent that they help us to 'define and argue out fundamental principles'. By way of example, Gandhi makes his point clear, "If some well-known character in religious books sinned against God or man, is that a warrant for our repeating the sin? It is enough for us to be told, once for all, that Truth is the only thing that matters in the world, that Truth is God. It is irrelevant to be told that even Yudhishthira was betrayed into an untruth" (*ibid*., 28). He observes that what is relevant for us is to know that when he spoke an untruth, he had to suffer for it that very moment. This is because his great name in no way protected him from punishment. Similarly, he takes note of the incident of Adi Shankara who avoided a *chandala*. For him, it is 'irrelevant' for us to be told that Adi Shankara avoided a *chandala*. In his view, what is to be noted is that a religion that teaches us to 'treat all that lives' cannot possibly countenance the inhuman treatment of a single creature, let alone a whole class of perfectly innocent human beings. Gandhi argues that we have not even 'all the facts' before us to judge what Adi Shankara did or did not do. In such an interpretation, he poses a semantic question. He asks, do we know the meaning of the word *chandala* where it occurs? He then replies, 'it has admittedly many meanings, one of which is a sinner'. Here he is trying to challenge the argument given in favour of untouchability based on Shastras by *Pandits*. He notes, " But if all sinners are to be regarded as untouchables, it is very much to be feared that we should all, not excluding the Pandit himself, be under the ban of untouchability"(*ibid*., 28). Gandhi takes a moral position and concludes that although untouchability is an old institution, it is an 'evil', and 'it cannot be defended on the ground of its antiquity' (*ibid*., 29).

He argues that 'Hinduism is and is not based on scriptures' (Gandhi, 1996: 5). In his view, Hinduism does not 'derive its authority from one book'. Although the *Gita* is universally accepted, even then, he notes, 'it only shows the way'. He observed, Hinduism is like the Ganga, which is pure and unsullied at its source and takes in the impurities along its path. Like the Ganga, Hinduism is also beneficent in its totality. It takes a provincial form in every province, but the inner substance is retained everywhere. He mentions that the purity of Hinduism depends on the self-restraint of its votaries rather than the words of the Shastra. His view on the Shastras is worth mentioning here. In his view, the Shastras are 'ever-growing'. He focuses on the 'time and context' in which the Shastras developed. He notes that the Vedas, the Upanishads, the Smritis, the Puranas, and the Itihasas did not arise at the same time. "Each grew out of the necessities of particular periods, and therefore they seem to conflict with one another" (*ibid*., 5-6). Thus, these books do not enunciate anew the eternal truths but show how these were practiced at the time to which the books belong. Consequently, a practice which was good enough in a particular period would, if blindly repeated in another, land people into the 'slough of despond'. Therefore, one cannot revive practices made earlier, such as animal sacrifice, eating beef, chopping off the hands and feet of thieves, polyandry, and child marriage. Doing them meant stagnation, and Hinduism abhors stagnation (*ibid*., 5-6).

Despite all these shortcomings, Gandhi believes in certain healthy conventions prevalent in Hinduism. One such convention is the recitation of the holy *shloka* like Gaytri. The convention is that it should be recited only at stated times and after ablutions performed in the prescribed manner. Even though he believes in this convention, he admits that he does not always follow it. He notes, "As I believe in those conventions, and as I am not able always to conform to them, for years past I have followed the later Saints, and therefore have satisfied myself with the Dwadashakshara Mantra of the Bhagavata or the still simpler formula of Tulsidas and a few selections from the *Gita* and other works, and a few bhajans in Prakrit. These are my daily spiritual food—my Gayatri. They give me all the peace and solace I need from day to day" (*ibid*., 11).

Gandhi also delves deeper into such discussion and points to the relationship between knowledge and truth in the context of Hinduism. He argues that knowledge is limitless and so also the application of truth. Thus, everyday we add to our knowledge of the power of Atman, and we shall keep on doing so. In his view, the new experience will teach us new duties, but the truth shall ever be the same. He poses the question, "Who has ever known it in its entirety? The Vedas represent the truth, they are infinite. But who has known them in their entirety? What goes today by the name of the Vedas are not even a millionth part of the real Veda—the Book of Knowledge. And who knows the entire meaning of even the few books that we have?" (*ibid*., 6). He offers a solution to this problem. In the face of these infinite complications, he notes Hindu sages taught us to learn one thing; 'As with the Self, so with the Universe'. It means: it is not possible to scan the universe: as it is to scan the self, i.e. know the self, and you know the universe. However, for Gandhi, even knowledge of the self within, presupposes ceaseless striving-not only ceaseless but pure, and pure striving presupposes a pure heart, which in turn depends on the practice of *yamas* and *niyamas*—the cardinal and casual virtues.

III

Despite the glorification of Hinduism, Gandhi is critical of certain practices inherent in it. One of such practices is the undue importance of the observance of eating practices among Hindus. He notes, 'Hindus have degraded their religion by making it simply the 'question of eating and drinking'. "Hinduism does not consist in eating and non-eating. Its kernel consists in right conduct, in the correct observance of truth and non-violence. Many a men eating meat, but observing the cardinal virtues of compassion and truth, and living in the fear of God, is a better Hindu than a hypocrite who abstains from meat. And he whose eyes are opened to the truth of the violence in beef-eating or meat-eating and who has therefore rejected them, who loves 'both man and bird and beast' is worthy of our adoration" (Gandhi, 1994: 26).

In his view, Hindus need to consider 'inward purity' rather than 'outward observances'. 'In the name of religion Hindus have made a fetish of outward observances and have degraded religion by making it simply a question of eating and drinking' (*ibid.*, 15). He warns, 'Hindus are doomed if they attach undue importance to the spiritual effects of foods and human contacts'. He further writes that bad and stimulating or dirty foods must be avoided like avoiding bad contact. However, these observances should not be given 'a place out of all proportion to their importance'. Instead, he observes, "Brahmanism owes its unrivalled position to its self-abnegation, its inward purity, its severe austerity—all these illuminated by knowledge" (*ibid.*, 15).

Second, he is also critical of the exaggerated notion of the influence of contact prevalent in Hinduism. He mentions that in our arrogance we exaggerate the influence of contact with people whom 'we often ignorantly and more often arrogantly consider to be our inferiors'. He says that before the Throne of the Almighty we shall be judged, not by what we have eaten nor by whom we have been touched by. Instead, we shall be judged by whom we have served and how. Since we serve a single human being in distress, we shall find favour in the sight of God. He was aware of many superstitions that go under the name of Hinduism. He wrote that he was 'painfully conscious of all the superstitions that are to be found masquerading as Hinduism, and he had no hesitation to call a spade a spade.' Describing repeatedly untouchability as the greatest of these superstitions, he noted that in spite of it, he would remain a Hindu. He argues he does not believe that these superstitions form part of Hinduism. In his words, "The very canons of interpretation laid down by Hinduism teach me that whatever is inconsistent with the truth....must be summarily rejected as not belonging to Hinduism" (*ibid.*, 47).

Gandhi also criticized the *Shuddhi* movement in Hinduism started by the Arya Samaj. He was against religious conversion or proselytism. He claims that there is no such thing as proselytism in Hinduism as it is understood in Christianity or to a lesser extent in Islam. The Arya Samaj, which started *shuddhi* and conversion, in Gandhi's view copied the

Christians in planning its propaganda. For him, these methods have done more harm than good. “Though regarded as a matter of the heart purely and one between the Maker and oneself, it has degenerated into an appeal to the selfish instinct” (*ibid.*, 19). He mentions that his ‘Hindu instinct’ tells him that all religions are more or less true. The reason is: all religions proceed from the same God and they all suffer from imperfect human instrumentality. In his view, ‘the real *shuddhi* movement should consist in each one trying to arrive at perfection in his or her own faith’ (*ibid.*, 19). In such a plan, character would be the only test. In his words, ‘conversion is like crossing from one compartment to another, if it does not mean a moral rise’ (*ibid.*, 19).

Let us see how Gandhi views the caste system of Hinduism. His views of the caste system have been constantly changing. In 1920, he saw it as ‘a method of social organization’ and ‘an extension of the principle of the family’ governed by ‘blood and heredity’ (CWMG 19: 175). He considered it as a ‘system of self-culture’ and the ‘best adaptation to social stability and progress’. However, he noted that the caste does not connote ‘superiority or inferiority’. In his opinion, it simply ‘recognizes different outlooks and corresponding modes of life’. However, he was aware that ‘a sort of hierarchy has been evolved in the caste system’ (CWMG 19 : 175). In 1921, he viewed the caste system from an economic point of view and noted it as ‘ensured hereditary skill’ and ‘a best remedy against pauperism’. Historically, he regarded caste as ‘man’s experiment or social adjustment in the laboratory of Indian society’ (Gandhi, 2008: 110). In 1925, he wrote that caste has ‘a scientific basis’ and it creates ‘a social and moral restraint’ (CWMG 26: 289). He explained in another context that the caste system was ‘a healthy division of work based on birth’ (CWMG 26: 540), but hastened to add that the ‘present ideas of caste were a perversion of the original’. Nor did he regard the abolition of restrictions on intermarriage and inter-dining as essential reforms. “These self-imposed restrictions have a sanitary as also a spiritual value. But non-observance no more dooms a man to perdition than its observance raises him to the seventh heaven” (CWMG 26:569). It was the principle of self-control implied in these restrictions that Gandhi valued most in traditional Brahmin culture. “I would not have the non-Brahmins to rise on the ruin of Brahmins. I would rather that they rose to the height that the Brahmins have occupied before now” (CWMG 26: 331). However, his position changed from the early 1920s. In 1931 he showed his disbelief in the caste system in the modern sense and found it as ‘an excrescence and a handicap on progress’ (CWMG 46:302). He also noted that caste connotes ‘distinctions in status’, and it is an ‘evil’ (CWMG 46:302).

Nevertheless, Gandhi later on in 1933 seems to have defended the caste system when Ambedkar attacked it. Responding to Ambedkar, he mentioned, "I do not believe in the caste system, even as distinguished from varnashrama, to be an 'odious and vicious dogma'. It has its limitations and its defects, but there is nothing sinful about it, as there is about untouchability, and, if it is a by-product of the caste system it is only in the same sense that an ugly growth is of a body, or weeds of a crop. It is as wrong to destroy caste because of the outcast, as it would be to destroy a body because of an ugly growth in it, or a crop because of the weeds" (CWMG 53: 26-61).

In 1936, he denied that the caste system had a religious basis. "Caste has nothing to do with religion. It is a custom whose origin I do not know, and do not need to know. But I do know that it is harmful, both to spiritual and national growth" (Gandhi, 1996: 12). With time, he turned more and more critical. He commented in 1946, 'Soil erosion eats up good soil. It is bad enough. Caste erosion is worse; it eats up men and divides men from men' (CWMG 84: 78). Gandhi never accepted the caste system as a valid Hindu practice in a religious and spiritual sense. In his view, the caste system had to be purified and corrected from the abusive and distorted form it had taken. His position was very clear; to reform and save Hinduism from its degraded state.

Besides his views on the caste system, his views on *Varnaashrama* are also worth mentioning. In 1921, he noted about *Varna* that it is the divisions that define 'duties' and confer 'no privileges'. "*Varnashrama* is, in my opinion, inherent in human nature, and Hinduism has simply reduced it to a science. It does attach to birth. A man cannot change his *varna* by choice" (CWMG 21: 246). He wrote, "All are born to serve God's creation—a *Brahmin* with his knowledge, a *Kshatriya* with his power of protection, a *Vaishya* with his commercial ability and a *Shudra* with bodily labour" (CWMG 21: 247). He also mentioned, "Varnashrama is self-restraint and conservation and economy of energy"(CWMG 21: 247).

In 1925, he noted, "*Varnashrama* is a dharma; the existence of many castes is not. Protecting the former is desirable; destruction of the latter is equally desirable" (CWMG 28: 14). In 1925, he further mentioned that religion is doomed to destruction which bases itself upon a system of gradations, high and low. He wrote, 'Such is not the meaning for me of *Varnashrama*'. For him, *Varnashrama* connotes 'an ideal system conceived for the highest good of society.' However, in the present time, he noted it has become 'a travesty and a mockery of the original' (CWMG 28 : 436). He commented in 1926 that although he did not believe in caste as it was at present constituted, he did believe in the 'four fundamental divisions' regulated according to the four principal occupations. He also pointed out that the existing innumerable divisions of castes, with the attendant artificial restrictions and elaborate ceremonial, are 'harmful to the growth of a religious spirit, as also to the social well-being of the Hindus and, therefore, also their neighbours' (CWMG 30: 47). In 1933, he stated *Varnashrama* is not 'a vertical section', but 'a horizontal plane'. It is such "a plane on which all stand on a footing of equality, doing the services respectively assigned to them. A life of religion is not a life of privileges but of duty" (CWMG 53: 258). In his view, *Varna* should not be confused with caste. In his words, "*Varna* has nothing to do with caste" (Gandhi, 1955: 168). And caste is an 'excrescence', just like untouchability, upon Hinduism'.

Gandhi is quite blunt, however, when he discusses untouchability.[3] As Kumarappa notes, "Even a reader well acquainted with Gandhi's writings may not realize that the topic on which he wrote and spoke most was the removal of untouchability. This fact reveals the supreme importance he attached to it" (Gandhi, 1954: iii). He viewed untouchability as 'an aberration' that had happened much later and was not a part of the original practice of *Sanatan dharma.* Earlier on 16 September, 1921, Gandhi in his speech to Labourers in Madras told that Untouchability is 'a sin against God and humanity' and 'a blot on Hinduism' (CWMG 21: 132). He was convinced that no religion worth its name could be guilty of such atrocities. Certainly not Hinduism which taught gentleness towards the cow and harmlessness even to the insect world. Untouchability is contrary to this essentially non-violent spirit of Hinduism. Thus, in his view, it must be cut out, root and branch, or Hinduism would perish.

He had strongly held the view that untouchability is 'an ineffaceable blot' that Hinduism today carries with it. He did not believe that it had been handed down from immemorial times. He writes, "I think that this miserable, wretched, enslaving spirit of untouchability must have come to us when we were in the cycle of our lives at our lowest ebb.... That any person should be considered untouchable in this sacred land, passes one's comprehension" (Gandhi, 1922: 326-37).

Gandhi, in 1933, again wrote in *Harijan*, "Untouchability as at present practiced is the greatest blot on Hinduism. It is (with apologies to sanatanists) against the Shastras. It is against the fundamental principles of humanity, it is against the dictates of reason that a man should, by mere reason of birth, be for ever regarded as an untouchable, even unapproachable and unseeable. These adjectives do not convey the full meaning of the thing itself. It is a crime for certain men, women and their children to touch, or to approach within stated distances, or to be seen by those who are called caste Hindus. The tragedy is that millions of Hindus believe in this institution as if it was enjoined by the Hindu religion" (CWMG 53: 262).

Gandhi believed that if untouchability was not dealt with, it could lead to the destruction of Hinduism itself. "I have said it several times, and shall repeat it today, that, unless we discharge our debt, Hinduism will perish. Untouchability must be destroyed, or else it will destroy Hinduism. That is why I am giving myself no rest. Not that I do not need it. I may say that I have several years of arrears of rest to cover, but how can I have rest? How can one have rest with a raging fire within? How can any Hindu, knowing that Hinduism is on the brink of an active volcano, afford to have a moment's rest?' (CWMG 60: 46-47). Gandhi informs why he considered untouchability as 'a curse', 'a blot', and a powerful 'poison' that will destroy Hinduism? He wrote in 1936, "It is repugnant to our sense of humanity to consider a single human being as untouchable by birth" (CWMG 63: 34). He claimed, "If you were to examine the scriptures of the world and the conduct of people other than Hindus, you do not find any parallel to untouchability" (CWMG 63: 34). Although Gandhi severely launched an attack on untouchability, he had very limited success.[4]

IV

Let us discuss the basis on which Gandhi launched an attack on the evil practices in Hinduism. There were two interrelated aspects to his attack on the worst aspects of the caste system and untouchability. He argued, on the one hand, that it was not in conformity with the basics of Hindu *Advaita* principles, and on the other socially and politically they were indefensible on moral grounds. His criticism of Hindu practices was based on Advaita Vedantic principles which served as the philosophical foundation for his Hinduism. He pointed out that as per *Advaita* all men were equal and the same because they were part of the same cosmic unity or divine.[5] He wrote, "I believe in *Advaita*, I believe in the essential unity of man and for that matter of all that lives. Therefore, I believe that if one man gains spiritually, the whole world gains with him and, if one man falls, the whole world falls to that extent" (CWMG 25: 390). His views on Hinduism are primarily based on his reading and understanding of the Hindu sacred text *Gita*.[6] He held that sacred texts like the *Gita*, when interpreted literally, depicted violence and untruth. Instead, he endeavoured to encourage a creative reading of these texts that would help situate Hinduism on the bedrock of truth and nonviolence. Through his interpretation, he attempted to give the ordinary Hindu reader the courage to treat this, hitherto considered sacred, not as something that was to be blindly worshipped or followed but as the embodiments of truth and non-violence. The central objective was to transport the reader of these texts to an ethical/spiritual plane. In his view, only this could make Hinduism an ethical religion.

Although he preferred the *Gita* as his favourite holy book, he felt that the essence of Hinduism can be found in the first verse of the *Ishopanishad*. Its impact was so powerful that he ventured to say that "the whole of Hinduism could be summed up in the first verse of *Ishopanishad*" (Gandhi, 1996: 21). Not only this he also suggested that 'if all other Hindu scriptures happened to be reduced to ashes and to go out of the memory of men and if only that one verse to abide with us, but the destruction would also be no loss. Hinduism would even then remain with us" (Gandhi, 1996: 21-22). He viewed it as 'one incredibly simple *mantra* of the *Ishopanishad*' that enjoys 'the sanctity of the Vedas' (Gandhi, 1996: 23). Gandhi regarded this *mantra* as an 'essence of Hinduism' (Gandhi, 1996: 23). This *mantra* is considered 'the bedrock of Hinduism' and without it Hinduism is nothing, and with it Hinduism requires nothing else. Further, 'anything that is inconsistent with the meaning of that *mantra* is not Hinduism' (CWMG 64: 259).

Gandhi mentioned that he read this *mantra* in the light of the *Gita* or the *Gita* in the light of the *mantra*. He found that the *Gita* is a commentary on this mantra. Moreover, in his views, it has the power to 'satisfy the cravings of the socialist and the communist, of the philosopher and the economist' (CWMG 64: 259). He notes that although he has been swearing by the *Bhagavadgita* and it answered all his difficulties and has been his '*kamadhenu*', his 'guide', his 'open sesame', but it is not a book that he can place before the whole of the audience (Gandhi, 1996: 19). The reason is that it takes prayerful study for '*Kamadhenu*' to yield the rich milk she holds in her udders. Thus, for the general audience or Hindus, it is the first verse of the *Ishopanishad* that 'contains the whole essence of Hinduism'.[7]

He offers the interpretation of this *mantra* in the following way: "Now this *mantra* divides itself into four parts (Gandhi, 1996: 20). The first part is *īśāvāsyam idaṃsarvaṃ yatkiñca jagatyāṃ jagat.* It means, as I would translate, "All this that we see in this great universe is pervaded by God.' Then come the second and third parts which read together, as I read them: *tena tyaktena bhuñjīthā* I divide these into two and translate them thus: 'Renounce it and enjoy it.' There is another rendering which means the same thing, though: 'Enjoy what He gives you.' Even so you can divide it into two parts. Then follows the final and most important part *mā gṛdhaḥ kasyasviddhanam* which means: 'Do not covet anybody's wealth or possession" (Gandhi, 1996: 20).

He comments that the three other parts of the *mantra* follow directly from the first. "If you believe that God pervades everything that He has created, you must believe that you cannot enjoy anything that is not given by Him. And seeing that He is the Creator of His numberless children, it follows that you cannot covet anybody's possession. If you think that you are one of His numerous creatures, it behoves you to renounce everything and lay it at His feet. That means that the act of renunciation of everything is not a mere physical renunciation but represents a second or new birth. It is a deliberate act, not done in ignorance. It is, therefore, a regeneration. And then since he who holds the body must eat and drink and clothe himself, he must naturally seek all that he needs from Him. And he gets it as a natural reward of that renunciation. As if this was not enough the *mantra* closes with this magnificent thought: Do not covet anybody's possession. The moment you carry out these precepts you become a wise citizen of the world living at peace with all that lives, it satisfies one's highest aspirations on this earth and hereafter" (*ibid.*, 21). It is this *mantra* that he described at another meeting as 'the golden key' for the solution of all the difficulties and doubts that may assail one's heart.

Gandhi also addresses non-Hindu critics, who only criticize Hinduism and catalogue its shortcomings. He wrote, these critics 'only blazon their own ignorance of Hinduism and their incapacity to regard it from the Hindu viewpoint' (CWMG 64: 332). This, in fact, 'distorts their vision and vitiates their judgment'. Yet, he argues that it is both their 'right and duty' to point out the defects in Hinduism to 'purify' it and to keep it pure' (CWMG 64: 332).

A distinguishing feature of Gandhi's interpretation of Hinduism is that he sets it in opposition to materialism and other civilizations. According to him, Hinduism teaches that the body is a limitation of the power of the soul within. He argues that as the West have made wonderful discoveries in material things, similarly Hinduism has made still more marvellous discoveries in the matter of religion, of the spirit, of the soul. But unfortunately, we have no eye for these great and fine discoveries. On the contrary, Hindus are dazzled by the material progress that Western science has made. Gandhi is not enamoured of that progress, but in his view, "God in His wisdom had prevented India from progressing along those lines, so that it might fulfil its special mission of resisting the onrush of materialism" (CWMG 35 : 524). At the same time, he notes that what we see today is not 'pure Hinduism', but often 'a parody' of it (CWMG 35: 524). "Otherwise it would require no pleading from me in its behalf, but would speak for itself, even as if I was absolutely pure I would not need to speak to you" (CWMG 35: 524).

After all, Gandhi argues, there is 'something' in Hinduism that is keeping it alive until now. "We have witnessed the fall of Babylonian, Syrian, Persian and Egyptian civilizations. On the other hand, Indian civilization persists... go through the most ancient records and then look round you and you would be constrained to say, "Yes, I see here ancient India still living" (CWMG 35: 525). He notes that it is true, there are 'dungheaps', too, here and there, but there are 'rich treasures' buried under them. In his view, the Indian civilization has survived because Hinduism has not developed along material but spiritual lines. Further, among its many contributions, the idea of man's identity with the dumb creation is a unique one of Hinduism. Then he mentions its contribution in men: Ramanuja, Chaitanya, Ramakrishna, not to speak of the more modern names who have 'left their impression on Hinduism' (CWMG 35: 525). He underlines the 'unique contribution' of Hinduism in the form of the four ashramas and claims that there is nothing like it in the whole world. He argues, "The Catholics have the order of celibates corresponding to *brahmacharis*, but not as an institution, whereas in India every boy had to go through the first *ashrama*. What a grand conception it was! Today our eyes are dirty, thoughts dirtier and bodies dirtiest of all, because we are denying Hinduism...Today varnashrama dharma and Hinduism are misrepresented and denied by its votaries. The remedy is not destruction, but correction. Let us reproduce in ourselves the true Hindu spirit, and then ask whether it satisfies the soul or not"(CWMG 35:524). Thus, he argues that Hinduism is by no means 'a spent force' or 'a dead religion' (CWMG 35: 525).

In an interview to Miss Fitch published in *Harijan* on 26 December, 1936, he noted that the "chief value of Hinduism lies in holding the actual belief that all life (not only human beings but all sentient beings) is one, i.e., all life coming from the One universal source, call it Allah, God or Parameshwara". He further mentioned that Hinduism excludes all exploitation. In his view, there is no limit whatsoever to the measure of sacrifice that one may make in order to realize this oneness with all life.

However, certainly the immensity of the ideal sets a limit to one's wants. Thus, Gandhi observes that one may see 'the antithesis of the position of modern civilization which says: 'Increase your wants'. On the contrary, he argues 'Hinduism rules out indulgence and multiplication of wants as these hamper one's growth to the ultimate identity with the Universal Self' (CWMG 64: 141).

Gandhi redefined Hinduism and gave it a more contemporary interpretation. The focus of this interpretation was not God, but men. Self-purification and active service in the spirit of love were also its contents. He rationalized Hinduism and reduced it to a set of such basic moral principles as love, truth, *ahimsa*, and social service. On the other hand, he marginalized the *Shastras* and deprived them of their religious and ethical authority. By the same token, he undermined the traditional religious basis of Brahmanic authority and liberated Hinduism from their stranglehold. It was based on his idea that every *yuga* had its own unique *dharma* and periodically needed to reinterpret the eternal moral principles.

NOTES

1. As part of this, we will mainly analyze Gandhi's compiled writings on Hinduism, *The Essence of Hinduism*. The text *The Essence of Hinduism* is compiled and edited by V.B. Kher and he points out in the preface of the text, it is 'so planned and arranged that each section naturally leads to the next one' (Gandhi, 1996: x). The editor also notes that "Gandhiji though not an *acharya* or an crudite scholar like Adi Shankaracharya, is the authentic voice of age-old Hinduism in modern times who has given it a new turn and direction" (Gandhi, 1996: ix).
2. He mentioned that the different religions were beautiful flowers from the same garden, or they were branches of the same majestic tree. Thus he claims that all religions are equally true, though being received and interpreted through human instruments equally imperfect.
3. Judith Brown has well summed up the Gandhian involvement with the problem of untouchability. She writes, "His primary social concern...was the problem of untouchability, the rejection of a whole group of the poorest and the most menial in society as a result of Hindu ideas of hierarchy, and purity and pollution. Now, as he travelled widely, he saw in harsh practice the power of this social division, and the poverty and degradation it caused, though he had rejected the whole idea far earlier and inveighed and worked against it even in South Africa. Once home in India, having tested the temper of public opinion, he was aware of the strength of Hindu orthodoxy and he took care not to equate his campaign against untouchability with

the question of caste as a whole for fear of holding back the work on what he saw as the most vital and urgent reform. Rather, he argued, his was a campaign to purify and strengthen caste by abolishing this pernicious custom. For Gandhi untouchability was primarily a religious problem. He believed that there was no warrant for it in the scriptures; it was a late and evil accretion which harmed and threatened the Hindu tradition he so treasured, and its observance was positively sinful. If it continued he feared that Hinduism would not survive. However, he was also clear that its observance impeded India's journey to *swaraj* at an obvious level, for such a profound fissure in Hindu society might well generate violent rebellion among untouchables against the higher castes, and would give leverage to any imperial authority wishing to maintain Indian divisions to rule" (see, Brown, 1992: 205-6).

4. Bhikhu Parekh has critically commented on the Gandhian programme on untouchability. He has pointed out one of the surprising aspect of it. He argues that the movement was not really organized along the lines of non-violent protest or satyagraha that Gandhi taught India and the world. Parekh argues, "Gandhi did more than any other Indian to undermine untouchability, yet his attack had a profound weakness. Gandhi saw it as a blot on the Hindu religion and made it the sole responsibility of the high caste Hindus to fight against it. The untouchables themselves, reduced to passive and pathetic symbols of high caste Hindu tyranny, were not involved in the struggle for their emancipation, a strange attitude in a man who everywhere else wanted the victims to fight for themselves. As a result, they had no opportunity to work and fight alongside the Hindus, and they neither occupied important positions in the *Harijan Sevak Sangh* and the Congress nor set up an independent and effective organization of their own. Not surprisingly they hardly grew under Gandhi's shadow, and a man who created so many great leaders was unable to create a single Harijan leader of equal stature. Ambedkar, one of the few exceptions, was not his favourite Harijan and grew in opposition to him" (see Parekh, 1991: 210-11).
5. It has been recently argued that Gandhi's writings suggest that he was not concerned to show faith in the fundamental principle of *Advaita* but to use or interpret the *Advaita* idea of oneness to argue that his idea of *varnashrama* does not accept any kind of superiority or inferiority between human beings. The word *Advaita* in Gandhi's writings shows his pragmatic use of the word evoking people's religious feeling and their faith in *Advaita* in support of his movement against untouchability.
6. Gandhi attempted to alter the vision of the ordinary Hindu by reinterpreting the *Bhagwad Gita*. By the middle of the 1920s, Gandhi had already acquired pan-Indian acceptability. His translation of the *Gita* started appearing in the columns of *Young India*, 1931. The translation and its introduction, called "Anasaktiyoga", was written for the ordinary people of India who, according to Gandhi "stand in need of its support". Gandhi introduces the *Gita* to them as an allegorical text and says that all the personalities that appear in it are products of the imagination of the author. His interpretation

of the *Gita* is quite different from others. In his interpretation, Gandhi criticizes the author for the thoughtless use of war imagery while, according to Gandhi, the central message of the text is *anasakti*. *Anasakti*, Gandhi argues, cannot be practiced without turning oneself first into a votary and practitioner of *ahimsa*. He also reinterprets *Bhakti* in such a way to make it synonymous with *ahimsa* and *Satya*. To remove the divine garb of Krishna, Gandhi treats him simply as a product of the author's imagination and cautions the reader against the folk tendency to take Krishna as a historical being. Gandhi also helps the ordinary reader to treat the *avatar* as a title given to a person who has done exemplary work for the community. Then he offers a brilliant ethical principle: That which cannot be done without selfishness ought to be rejected as evil.

7. Gandhi also offers the short version of this *mantra* as following; "The very first verse of the *Ishopanishad* means simply this: God pervades everything that is to be found in this universe down to the tiniest atom. The *mantra* describes God as the Creator, the Ruler, and the Lord. The seer to whom this *mantra* or verse was revealed was not satisfied with the magnificent statement that God was to be found everywhere. But he went further and said: "Since God pervades everything nothing belongs to you, not even your own body" (Gandhi, 1996:19).

REFERENCES

Brown, Judith. (1992). *Gandhi: Prisoner of Hope*. New Delhi: Oxford University Press.

Gandhi, M.K. (1922). *Speeches and Writings of Mahatma Gandhi*. Madras: G.K. Nasan and Co.

Gandhi, M.K. (1954). *The Removal of Untouchability* (ed.B Kumarrapa). Ahmedabad: Navajivan.

Gandhi, M.K. (1955). *My Religion*. Ahmedabad: Navajivan.

Gandhi, M.K. (1996). *The Essence of Hinduism*. Ahmedabad: Navajivan.

Gandhi, M.K. (1994). *What is Hinduism*. New Delhi: National Book Trust.

Parekh, Bhikhu. (1991). *Gandhi's Political Philosophy: A Critical Examination*. London: Palgrave Macmillan.

Prabhhu, R.K and U.R. Rao. (2008). *The Mind of Mahatma*. Ahmedabad: Navajivan.

The Collected Works of Mahatma Gandhi Vol.1-100 (CWMG-KS-1956-1994), New Delhi: Publication Division, The Government of India. Retrieved from *https://www.gandhiheritageportal.org/. CWMG Vol.1- 100.* The Collected Works of Mahatma Gandhi (CWMG Vol. 1-100) is a standard source of Gandhi's writings and speeches. This one-time authentic documentation of Gandhi's available writings was carried out meticulously, and conscientiously under the CWMG project of the Government of India in 1956. The author has used the CWMG-KS-1956-1994 edition in this study.

5
Ambedkar's *Philosophy of Hinduism*

Hinduism! Thy name is inequality,

(Ambedkar, BAWS 3: 87)

In our second chapter, we noted Ambedkar's critique of Hinduism through his autobiographical narrative *Waiting for a Visa*. We saw how he was humiliated because of the practice of untouchability found in Hinduism. We further observed that Ambedkar saw such humiliation, not only as a sporadic and occasional event, but inherent and institutionalized in Hinduism itself. This chapter focuses on his seminal work, *Philosophy of Hinduism*, to explore his philosophical analysis of Hinduism in more depth.[1] We will also briefly examine his other works on Hinduism: *The Hindu Social Order: Its Essential Principles*, *The Hindu Social Order: Its Unique Features*, *Riddles in Hinduism*, and *Annihilation of Caste* in order to gain a more comprehensive understanding of his critique.

Ambedkar's *Philosophy of Hinduism* is a highly scholastic text. He begins his inquiry with a question: what is the philosophy of Hinduism? He notes that it is a question which arises in 'its logical sequence' and its 'importance can never be omitted from consideration' (BAWS 3: 3). Further, 'without it no one can understand the aims and ideals of Hinduism'. He argues that 'such a study must be preceded by a certain amount of what may be called clearing of the ground and defining of the terms involved' (*ibid.*, 3). He thus examines the approach to the subject before analyzing Hindu philosophy. He uses the philosophical method of critical inquiry to comprehend the meaning of concepts and terms related to religion and philosophy in general, and to Hinduism in particular. For instance, he writes that one must define what he understands by religion as there is 'no agreement as to its exact definition' (*ibid.*, 5). Thus, in the initial part of the text, he elaborately defines key terms and concepts like religion, theology, philosophy, philosophy of religion, God, its relation to men and society in a highly scholastic manner. Further, in his philosophical analysis of Hinduism, he uses the academic insights gained from his ardent studies of philosophy, history, anthropology, and sociology. Combining the insights of these social sciences, he employs a multi-disciplinary approach to study, understand, and critically evaluate Hinduism.

In order to engage in a systematic analysis of the question, he attempts to seek clarity on two particular terms: philosophy and religion as well as their relationship. He takes note of the different use of the terms philosophy, religion and philosophy of religion. He claims that his use of the term philosophy refers to the 'teachings of great thinkers such as Socrates, Plato and so on'. "I am using the word Philosophy in its original sense which was two-fold. It meant teachings as it did when people spoke of the philosophy of Socrates or the philosophy of Plato. In another sense it meant critical reason used in passing judgments upon things and events" (*ibid.*, 5). He argues, while religion is something definite, there is nothing definite in philosophy. Combining Philosophy and Religion means, as he notes, 'an analysis and interpretation of the experience in question in the bearing upon our view of man, and the world in which he lives' (*ibid.*, 4). He claims that he uses the term 'philosophy of religion' in the sense of a descriptive and normative science. According to him, "Philosophy of religions to me... is both descriptive as well as normative. In so far as it deals with the teaching of a Religion, Philosophy of religion becomes a descriptive science... in so far as it involves the use of critical reason for passing judgment on those teachings, it is a normative science" (*ibid.*, 5). He further notes, "From this it will be clear what I shall be concerned within this study of the Philosophy of Hinduism. To be explicit I shall be putting Hinduism on its trial to assess its worth as away of life" (*ibid.*, 5).

Having clarified the different terms, he focuses on the context of the discussion and use of the term. He notes that he uses the term religion to mean theology in his discussion and further limits theology to natural theology. Taking the three theses of Theology, namely (1) the existence of God, (2) God's providential government of the universe, and (3) God's moral government of mankind, he takes religion to mean 'the propounding of an ideal scheme of divine governance the aim and object of which is to make the social order in which men live a moral order.' 'This is what I understand by Religion and this is the sense in which I shall be using the term Religion in this discussion' (*ibid.*, 6).

Having insisted the necessity of a philosophical criterion, Ambedkar suggests that a philosophy of a religion must be judged, based on its 'revolution' because the mother of Philosophy is revolution. As he notes, "Revolution is the mother of philosophy and if it is not the mother of philosophy, it is a lamp, which illuminates philosophy. Religion is no exception to this rule. The best method to ascertain the criterion of which to judge the philosophy of (any) religion is to study the Revolutions which religion has undergone. That is the method I propose to adopt" (*ibid.*, 8). He clarifies that revolution is to be both a conceptual and social in nature. By social revolution, he means alternative changes in structures of society towards an egalitarian social order. If any religion does not pass the test of 'such revolutions' both theoretical and social then, he argues, it tends to be not positivistic.

Setting revolution as one of the criteria for an analysis of religion, Ambedkar proceeds to classify two different types of religion—the religion of the Savage society and the religion of the civilized society. In the religion of the civilized society, he introduces two sub-divisions—the religion of antique or ancient society and the religion of the modern society. He notes that the religion of the savage society does not permit itself to undergo any radical theoretical revolution. It is only 'concerned with life and the preservation of life and it is these life processes which constitute the substance and source of the religion of savage society' (*ibid.*, 10). Religion of the Savage Society primarily focuses on the fact of human existence through ritualistic, ceremonial, magical, and fetishistic practices such as life, death, birth etc.

In contrast, the religion of the civilized society has the potential for conceptual revolution. Ambedkar distinguishes two stages of the religion of the civilized society; the religion of the antique society and the religion of the modern society. Religion in antique society was based on the bond of kinship between God and his worshippers. In ancient society, God was conceived to be 'the father of his people' but the basis of this conception of Fatherhood was deemed to be physical, and particular. While in modern society, 'the idea of divine-fatherhood has become entirely dissociated from the physical basis of natural fatherhood' (*ibid.*, 16). In its place, man is conceived to be created in the image of God. He argues that in modern society the idea of God has emerged as the creator and governor of the universe. He has an absolute status both morally and existentially. The modern or civilized world has envisioned a morally based humanity.

Clarifying the features of religions of savages and modern society, and specifying that revolution is one of the touchstones that can measure the progress of religion, Ambedkar then proceeds on to list the other normative criteria for judging the authenticity of a religion. These criteria are the concepts of Utility and Justice. His idea of an antique society leads him to adopt utility as a criterion of religion. Similarly, he claims that the concept of justice is derived from the idea of modern society. He says, "At the one hand of the revolution was the antique society with its religious ideal in which the end is the society. At the other end of revolution is the modern society with its religious ideal in which the end is the individual. To put the same fact in terms of the norm, it can be said that the norm or criterion for judging right or wrong in the antique society is Utility while the norm or the criterion for judging right or wrong in the modern society is Justice' (*ibid.*, 22).

Having set the background, it is in Part III of the text that Ambedkar begins his analysis of the philosophy of Hinduism. He notes that religion plays a significant role in a Hindu's life. He offers how a Hindu life style is influenced by his religion. He writes, "The life of the Hindu is regulated by Religion at every moment of his life. It orders him how during life he should conduct himself and how on death his body shall be disposed of. It tells him how and when he shall indulge in his sexual impulses. It tells him what ceremonies are to be performed when a child is born—how he should name, how he should cut the hair on its head, how he should perform its first feeding. It tells him what occupation he can take to, what woman he should marry. It tells him with whom he should dine and what food he should eat, what vegetables are lawful and what are forbidden. It tells how he should spend his day, how many times he should eat, how many times he should pray. There is no act of the Hindu which is not covered or ordained by Religion" (*ibid.*, 23). He also notes that religion is a 'social force' which stands for 'a scheme of divine governance'. The scheme becomes an ideal for society to follow. In his view, religious ideals hold sway over mankind, regardless of any earthly gain. Moreover, 'A religious ideal never fails to work so long as there is faith in that ideal'. Thus, 'To ignore religion is to ignore a live wire'.

Ambedkar offers 'the inquiry into the philosophy of Hinduism' from which 'there is no escape'. He applies two tests, as mentioned earlier, the test of justice and the test of utility to judge the philosophy of Hinduism. He considers justice as 'another name for liberty, equality and fraternity'. He poses a question: which of these tenets does Hinduism recognize? Does Hinduism recognize Equality?

He responds, "The question instantaneously brings to one's mind the caste system. One striking feature of the caste system is that the different castes do not stand as a horizontal series all on the same plane. It is a system in which the different castes are placed in a vertical series one above the other" (*ibid.*, 25).

Ambedkar points out 'the rules of sacraments' in Hinduism in which 'there lies the spirit of inequality'. Outlining and analyzing *Manusmirti*, he argues that in Hinduism you will find both social inequality and religious inequality imbedded in its philosophy. 'To prevent man from purifying himself from sin!! To prevent man from getting near to God!' He invites us to see how such rules are abominable and an indication of a perverse mind. He observes it as a 'glaring instance' of how Hinduism is a denial not only of equality but also of denial of the sacred character of human personality.

Again he puts a question as to: does Hinduism recognize liberty? He argues that liberty to be real must be accompanied by certain 'social conditions'. The social conditions include social equality, economic security and knowledge made available to all. He examines all three conditions through textual analysis of *Manusmirti*.

For him, Hinduism is not only about social inequality but economic inequality also. He proceeds to elaborate on economic security and notes 'three things' that shine out in Hinduism. First, Hinduism denies freedom of a vocation. In the Scheme of Manu, he observes, each man has his vocation preordained for him before he is born (*ibid.*, 39). Thus, Hinduism allows no choice. Additionally, since the occupation is predetermined, it has no relationship to the individual's capacity or inclination. Second, Hinduism compels people to serve ends chosen by others. For instance, Manu tells the Shudra that he was born to serve the higher classes. Third, Hinduism leaves no scope for the Shudra to accumulate wealth. Thus, in Hinduism, he notes, there is no choice of occupation. There is no economic independence and there is no economic security. In the matter of the spread of knowledge, he points out two conditions as prerequisites; formal education and literacy. Without these two, he mentions, knowledge cannot spread.

How does Hinduism stand in this matter? He argues that the concept of formal education in Hinduism was of a very limited character. It was confined only to the study of the Vedas. He says that it was 'natural' as for the Hindus there was 'no knowledge outside the Vedas'. Thus, the formal education was confined to the study of the Vedas. Second, formal education was to be taken in the schools established for the study of the Vedas. He argues that these schools benefited only the Brahmins. On the other hand, the State did not consider itself responsible for opening establishments for the study of arts and sciences. Thus, in his view, Hinduism, far from encouraging spread of knowledge, is a 'gospel of darkness' (*ibid.*, 44). On this basis, he notes that Hinduism is opposed to the conditions in which liberty can thrive. Hinduism is, therefore, a denial of liberty.

Does Hinduism recognize fraternity? Before dealing with this question, he sets a framework for analysis pointing to two forces prevalent in society; individualism and fraternity. Individualism is ever present. Every individual under the pressure of his own particular interests acts as an end and thereby develops a non-social and even an antisocial self. On the other hand, he argues, fraternity is a 'force of opposite character'. It is another name for fellow feeling. It is a sentiment which leads an individual to identify himself with the good of others whereby 'the good of other becomes to him a thing naturally and necessarily to be attended to like any of the physical conditions of our existence' (*ibid.*, 44). It is because of this sentiment of fraternity that the individual does not "bring himself to think of the rest of his fellow-creatures as struggling rivals with him for the means of happiness, whom he must desire to see defeated in their object in order that he may succeed in his own" (*ibid.*, 44). He mentions that individualism would produce anarchy and it is only fraternity which will prevent it and help to sustain the moral order among men.

Having set the framework, he raises the question again: does this sentiment of fellow feeling find a place among the Hindus? He provides 'facts' to shed light on this issue. In his words, "The first fact that strikes one is the number of castes. Nobody has made an exact computation of their number. But it is estimated that the total is not less than 2000. It might be 3000. This is not the only distressing aspect of this fact. There are others. Castes are divided into sub-castes. Their number is legion. The total population of the Brahmin Caste is about a crore and half. But there are 1886 sub-castes of the Brahmin Caste. In the Punjab alone the Saraswat Brahmins of the Province of Punjab are divided into 469 sub-castes. The Kayasthas of Punjab are divided into 590 sub-castes. One could go on giving figures to show this infinite process of splitting social life into small fragments. The third aspect of this splitting process is the infinitely small fragments into which the Castes are split. Some of the Baniya sub-castes can count no more than 100 families. They are so inter-related they find extremely difficult to marry within their castes without transgressing the rules of consanguinity" (*ibid.*, 45).

Ambedkar highlights the division of social life within Hinduism. He underlines the hierarchical nature of the Caste System.Castes form hierarchies in which one caste is at the top and is the highest whereas another is at the bottom and is the lowest. Moreover, in between there are castes everyone of which is at once above some castes and below some castes. He raises the question of graded hierarchy in Hinduism and writes that the caste system is a system of gradation in which every caste except the highest and the lowest has a priority and precedence over some other caste. Investigating how the precedence or the superiority is determined, he notes, this order of superiority and inferiority is determined by two Rules—(a) which are connected with religious rites, and (b) which are connected with commensuality. In his view, religion as a basis of the Rules of precedence manifests itself in three ways. Firstly, through religious ceremonies, secondly, through chants that accompany the religious ceremonies and thirdly through the position of the priest.

Ambedkar's central concern is that caste prevents social mobilization. He argues that there are 'certain occasions arise when society must mobilize all its resources to save itself from a catastrophe for instance war' (*ibid.*, 71). For such a situation, he notes, society must mobilize all its resources for militarization. He mentions that in such a situation, everyone must go to war and be a soldier. Is this possible under the theory of caste? Obviously not, he holds. Hence, he argues, the defeat India has suffered throughout history is due to caste. Caste prevented general mobilization. Further, the extent of mobilization had also been of a very limited character. The Kshatriyas were the only ones expected to fight. The Brahmins and Vaishyas did not have weapons, and the Shudras, who constituted a large majority in the country, were disarmed. The result, Ambedkar notes, was that once the small class of Kshatriyas was defeated by a foreign enemy the whole country fell at his feet. It could offer no resistance. It was not capable of resistance. Indian wars have been mostly wars of single battles or single campaigns. This was due to the fact that once the Kshatriyas got defeated, everything fallen. As a result, the Indians' continued defeat could be attributed to the theory deeply ingrained in the psyche of people and lack of general mobilization. He concludes, "how can a philosophy which dissects society in fragments, which dissociates work from interest, which disconnects intelligence from labour, which expropriates the rights of man to interests vital to life and which prevented society from mobilizing resources for common action in the hour of danger, be said to satisfy the test of Social Utility. The Philosophy of Hinduism therefore neither satisfies the test of social utility nor does it satisfy the test of individual justice" (*ibid.*, 71).

Ambedkar in his analysis attempts to show the deeper problem of Hinduism itself. Hinduism is, for him, the gospel of the superman. It teaches that what is right for the superman is the only thing which is called morally right and morally good. In his view, 'Manu's is a degraded and degenerate philosophy of superman as compared with that of Nietzsche and therefore far more odious and loathsome than the philosophy of Nietzsche. This explains why the philosophy of Hinduism does not satisfy the test of justice or of utility. He notes that Hinduism is not interested in the common man' (*ibid.*, 77). It is also not interested in society as a whole. The centre of its interest actually lies in a particular class and its philosophy. It is only concerned with sustaining and supporting the rights of that class. That is why in the Philosophy of Hinduism the interests of the common man as well as of society are denied, suppressed and sacrificed to the interests of this class of Supermen. In short, the philosophy of Hinduism is such that it cannot be called the Religion of humanity. It does not vitrify the inner life of ordinary humanity. In addition, if it does anything, it paralyzes it. In Hinduism, there is no nourishment for ordinary human souls, no comfort for ordinary human sorrow, and no help for ordinary human weakness. He observes that it leaves men in darkness face to face with the 'unthinking energies of nature'. 'Not less cruel than the crudest irreligion, does it leave men divorced from all communion with God'. Such is the philosophy of Hinduism. He notes that it is 'Superman's heaven and the common man's damnation' (*ibid.*, 78).

Before concluding his text Philosophy of Hinduism, Ambedkar turns back to the three terms with which he began his text philosophy, religion and philosophy of religion. He forcefully asserts that the philosophy of Hinduism fails to uphold the ideals of the three distinct terms. It is a set of doctrines marred with instances of inequality, favouritism, social and spiritual disintegration of a man and his community. In his outburst against Hinduism as a religion, he also states that he follows the lead of Edmund Burke on the necessity of religion as a set of doctrines for governance. He supplements his argument by citing doctrines intrinsic to Hinduism, thus, painting a real, rational and unapologetic picture of Hinduism. One may note his emphasis seems to be more on the articulation of a problem than conceptualizing a solution.

Ambedkar concludes his argument by stating that the philosophy of Hinduism fails to uphold both the ideals of social utility and individual justice. He accuses Hinduism of keeping the Shudras and the Untouchables in the dark for generations. To answer again why Hinduism fails the trial, he explains that while community and individual formed the core of savage society and civilised society respectively, Hinduism takes into consideration only the socio-political interests of one particular class, the Brahmins, and therefore fails to uphold any constructive, constitutive ideal. Though Ambedkar quotes largely from the *Manusmriti* and the verse of "*Purushasukta*," he defends his choice of sacred texts by stating that the horrors of the caste system are entrenched in the Vedas, Upanishads and the *Gita* as well. Ambedkar sums up the *Gita* as '...Manu in a nutshell'. He writes, "The Brahmins who were the authors of the whole body of Hindu Religious Literature—except the Upanishad Literature—took good care to inject the doctrines formulated by them in the Smritis, into the Vedas and the *Bhagwad Gita*. Nothing is to be gained in picking and chosing between them. The Philosophy of Hinduism will be the same whether one takes the *Manusmriti* as its Gospel or whether one takes the Vedas and the *Bhagwad Gita* as the gospel of Hinduism (*ibid*., 81).

He summarizes the argument stating, "Inequality is the soul of Hinduism. The morality of Hinduism is only social. It is unmoral and unhuman to say the least. What is unmoral and unhuman easily becomes immoral, inhuman and infamous. This is what Hinduism has become. Those who doubt this or deny this proposition should examine the social composition of the Hindu Society and ponder over the condition of some of the elements in it" (*ibid*., 87).

Ambedkar in another work, *The Hindu Social Order: Its Essential Principles* analyzes the Hindu social order. He begins with a question: Is it (Hindu Social Order) a free social order? (BAWS 3: 95). He argues in his text that the Hindu social order does not recognize the individual as a centre of social purpose. It is based primarily on class or Varna and not on individuals. Originally and formally the Hindu social order recognized four classes: (1) Brahmins, (2) Kshatriyas, (3) Vaishyas, and (4) Shudras. Today it consists of five classes, the fifth being called the Panchamas or Untouchables. The unit of Hindu society is not the individual Brahmin or the individual Kshatriya or the individual Vaishya or the individual Shudra or the individual Panchama. In this social order, even the family is not the unit of society except for the purposes of marriage and inheritance. The unit of Hindu society is the class or Varna. He mentions that it might be in technical term called class. Further, in the Hindu social order, individual merit and individual justice are not significant. If the individual has a privilege it is not personal but the privilege goes with the class. Thus if one enjoy it, it is because he belongs to that class. Contrawise, if an individual is suffering from a wrong, it is not because he by his conduct deserves it. The disability is the disability imposed upon the class and if he is found to be labouring under it, it is because he belongs to that class. Analyzing the Hindu social order, he questions; does the Hindu social order recognize fraternity? The Hindus like the Christians and the Muslims do believe that men are created by God. But while the Christians and the Muslims accept this as the whole truth, the Hindus believe that this is only part of the truth. According to them, the whole truth consists of two parts. The first part is that men are created by God. The second part is that God created different men from different parts of his divine body. Invoking *Purushasukta* of Hindu scripture, he mentions, the Hindus regard the second part as more important and more fundamental than the first. The Hindu social order is based on the doctrine that men are created from the different parts of the divinity. According to this doctrine, the Brahmin is no brother to the Kshatriya because the former is born from the mouth of the divinity while the latter is from the arms. The Kshatriya is no brother to the Vaishya because the former is born from the arms and the latter from his thighs. As no one is a brother to the other, no one is the keeper of the other. He argues that this doctrine has created an instinct of 'difference' and 'separateness'. In his words, "The doctrine that the different classes were created from different parts of the Divine body has generated the belief that it must be divine will that they should remain separate and distinct. It is this belief which has created in the Hindu an instinct to be different, to be separate and to be distinct from the rest of his fellow Hindus" (*ibid*., 100). Does the Hindu social order recognize equality? Relating it to fraternity, he argues the fundamental condition for the growth of the sentiment of fraternity is not preaching that we are children of God or the realization that one's life is dependent upon others. But the condition for the growth of this sentiment of fraternity lies in sharing in the vital processes of life. It is sharing in the joys and sorrows of birth, death, marriage and food. Thus the answer to the question of equality in the Hindu social order is negative (*ibid*., 106).

Ambedkar shows the flaws of the Hindu social doctrine. In his view, the doctrine 'men are born equal' is in opposition to the Hindu social order. According to the Hindu social order, men are the children of Prajapati the Creator of the Universe. However, they were created from the different parts of the body of Prajapati. This constructs an inherent contradiction in Hindu social doctrine. He notes that the Hindu social order is not based on equality and fraternity, and examines the principles on which it is based. In his view, the Hindu social order is reared on three principles. The first and foremost of these is the principle of graded inequality (*ibid*., 106). The principle of graded inequality is a fundamental principle and it is beyond controversy. The four classes are not on a horizontal plane but on a vertical plane. Further, they are not only different but unequal in status, one standing above the other. This order of precedence among the classes is not merely conventional. It is spiritual, moral and legal. There is no sphere of life which is not regulated by this principle of graded inequality. He argues that the principle of graded inequality has been implemented in the economic field also. The Hindu social order does not believe in 'from each according to his ability; to each according to his need' but 'From each according to his need. To each according to his nobility' (*ibid.*, 111). The Hindu social order does not identify equal need, equal work or equal ability as the basis of reward for labour. Its axiom is that in regard to the allocation of the pleasant things of life those who are reckoned as the highest must get the most and the finest. On the other hand, those who are the lowest must accept the least and the worst.

The second principle of Hindu social order is the 'fixity of occupations for each class and continuance thereof by heredity' (*ibid.*, 111).

The third principle on which the Hindu social order is founded is the fixation of people within their respective classes (*ibid.*, 113). He argues that there is nothing strange about it. Everywhere there are classes and no society is without them. Even a free social order will not be able to get rid of the classes. His basic concern is that so long as the classes practice isolation and exclusiveness, they are only non-social in their relations towards one another. "Isolation makes for rigidity of class consciousness, for institutionalizing social life and for the dominance of selfish ideals within the classes. Isolation makes life static, continues the separation into a privileged and underprivileged, masters and servants" (*ibid.*, 113). He sums up his arguments as follows, "...the Hindu social order is an order based on classes and not on individual. It is an order in which classes are graded one above the other. It is an order in which the status and functions of the classes are determined and fixed. The Hindu social order is a rigid order. No matter what changes take place in the relative position of an individual his social status as a member of the class he is born in relation to another person belonging to another class shall in no way be affected. The first shall never become the last. The last shall never become the first" (*ibid.*, 115).

In Chapter 3 of the volume 3 titled 'The Hindu Social Order: Its Unique Features' notes that the Hindu social order has some unique features (BAWS 3: 116). These unique features are as significant as the essentials. 'No study of the Hindu social order which does not make any reference to them can be regarded as complete or accurate.' In his view, the special features of the Hindu social order are three in number. Among these three, the worship of the superman or Brahmin is most striking. In this respect, the Hindu social order is nothing but Nietzsche's Gospel put into action. Quoting Manusmirti, he says, "The Brahmin or the Superman of the Hindu social order was entitled to certain privileges. In the first place, he could not be hanged even though he might be guilty of murder" (*ibid.*, 118).

By citing Hindu texts, Ambedkar illustrates the privileges of Brahmins, the supermen. The superman could take the property of the common man (the Shudra) without compensation. It could be done without involving the court, if that was necessary for the performance of his religious duties. Further, if Superman discovers a hidden treasure, he was free to appropriate the whole of it without giving the usual share to the king. This was 'since he was the lord of all' and was allowed to claim half, if it was discovered by another. He was entitled to the whole amount accumulated from legal fines from a king, whose death was due to some incurable disease. He was exempted from taxation also. He was entitled to compel the king to provide for his daily food and to see that he did not starve. His property was 'free from the law of escheat' (*ibid.*, 120). The superman of the Hindu social order is not bound by the rules as to occupation, if he is in distress. The privileges of the superman are not at all countersbalanced by an obligation towards the common man. In fact, the superman has no duty toward the common man. He is not bound to do charity for the uplift of the common man. On the other hand, receiving charity is the monopoly of Superman. For any other person to receive charity is a sin. To the common man (Shudra) who is born to serve the Superman man, the Superman is not at all required to be a good employer and is 'not bound to keep him well-fed, well clothed and well-housed' (*ibid.*, 121). The rise of the common man is antagonistic to the supremacy of Superman. In order to keep the Superman satisfied, happy and secure the Hindu social order takes 'special care to keep the Common man in a state of perpetual degradation' (*ibid.*, 121).

Similarly, Ambedkar questions the purpose of the ashram life prescribed in Hinduism. A Hindu's life is divided into four periods. The first period is called *Brahmacharya*, the stage of a student. The second period is known as *Grahasthashram*, the stage of married life. The third period is referred to as *Vanasprastha*, the stage of detachment from worldly life. The fourth period is called *Sanyasa* which is complete severance from the affairs of the world which is tantamount to civil death. The common man, Shudra, is denied the right to be a Sanyasi. The reason for such denial is to benefit Superman. Ambedkar argues, a Shudra by becoming a Sanyasi ceases to render service to Superman. Further, "A Shudra by becoming a Sanyasi reaches God or *Brahma* which is an invasion of the privileges of Superman" (*ibid*., 123). Further, citing Manu, Ambedkar claims that the Hindu social order is openly and avowedly devised and intended for the good of the Brahman—the Superman. In it everything is ordained for Superman. Superman has rights but no duties. Superman has everything at his disposal, and he must assign everything to his benefit. The counterpart of the same feature is the degradation of the common man—Shudra. As against Superman, the common man has no right to life, liberty, property or the pursuit of happiness. He must be ready to sacrifice everything for the sustenance of the life and dignity of Superman. The Hindu social order prescribes that such sacrifice should be made willingly by the common man. Indeed, it inculcates that the common man should respond to such call for sacrifice in the interest of Superman as his supreme duty (*ibid*., 123).

A second feature of preserving the Hindu Social Order is to deny the opportunity to rise, the right to education, and the right to use arms. This is in order to prevent rebellion against the social order. The Hindu social order has adopted this method to fix the social status of the lower orders for all generations to come. Their economic status is also fixed. There being no disparity between the two, there is no possibility of a grievance growing up. It has denied education to the lower orders. The result is that no one is conscious of their low condition. If there is any awareness, it is that nobody is responsible for the poor condition. It is 'the result of fate' (*ibid*., 126). The third special feature of the Hindu social order is that it is a 'Divine order' designed by God himself. 'As such it is sacred, not open to abrogation, amendment, not even to criticism' (*ibid*., 128). He mentions that it is not only a 'special feature' of the Hindu social order, but an 'extraordinary feature'. 'An examination of consecrations will show that there are instances where society has consecrated inanimate beings and inculcated on the minds of its members the religious belief that they are sacred' (*ibid*., 128). He noted the Hindus are the only people in the world whose social order—the relation of man to man—is consecrated by religion and made divine, eternal and inviolate. 'The Hindus are the only people in the world whose economic order—the relation of workman to workman—is consecrated by religion and made sacred, eternal and inviolate' (*ibid*., 128).

In Volume 4 of BAWS, we further note Ambedkar's views on Hinduism. It mostly deals with the 'Riddles' of Hinduism.[2] He believes that in the Hindu social order or in Hinduism, there are many mysterious things which one cannot explain. These are the riddles in Hinduism. According to him, there are around 24 riddles in Hinduism. These riddles obstruct the path of inquiry and without inquiry there can be no knowledge. Through these riddles, he wished to develop a rational approach to the social and religious problems of Hinduism. The introduction notes that it is "an exposition of the beliefs propounded by what might be called Brahmanic theology. It is intended for the common mass of Hindus who need to be awakened to know in what quagmire the Brahmins have placed them and to lead them on to the road of rational thinking" (BAWS 4: 5). Dealing with all the riddles is not possible in this study but two riddles may be explained here to demonstrate the intensity of Ambedkar's critique of Hinduism.

The riddle one deals with 'The Difficulty of knowing why one is Hindu' (BAWS 4: 13). He writes that India is a congeries of communities like Parsis, Christians, Mohammedans and Hindus. Now, if a Parsi is asked why he is so, he will answer that it is because he is a follower of Zoraster. The same holds true for a Muslim. He will say that he is a follower of Allah, and thus a Muslim. But when the same question is asked to a Hindu and if he says that he worships the same God as his community does, his answer cannot be true. This is because all Hindus do not worship the same God. There are divisions of Hindus as well—monotheists, polytheists, and pantheists where monotheists believe that there is only one God. Polytheists believe that there is more than one God and pantheists worship all the Gods including Vishnu, Shiva, Rama, Krishna, Kali, Parvati, Laxmi etc. If someone says that he is a Hindu because he holds the same beliefs as other Hindus, his answer is not right. This is because Hinduism has no definite creed and there is a complex collection of creeds and doctrines in Hinduism. It shelters people who propitiate their deity by bloody sacrifices. If someone claims that he is a Hindu because he follows the same customs as other Hindus, then also he is wrong, as all Hindus do not follow the same customs. In the North, near relatives are forbidden to marry whereas in the South, cousin marriage is allowed. There are places where people make it a rule to dedicate a daughter—and sometimes, sons—to a life of religious prostitution in the name of Devdasi. We can clearly see that Hinduism is not based on one particular God. It exploits the lower classes in the name of the 'caste system'. The managers of this religion, i.e. the Brahmins decide what the other castes can do and what cannot. They decide who can go to the temple and who cannot. Even in earlier times, it was also decided by the Brahmins who could take education and who cannot. Even Brahmins do not worship the same God. It is ridiculous that most followers of Hinduism cannot answer this simple question, "Why is he a Hindu?" thus this riddle remains unsolved.

In the riddle two titled 'The Origin of Vedas', Ambedkar discusses some of the most intriguing riddles connected with the Vedas. He develops other riddles also out of it. The Vedas are the sacred books of the Hindus. There is hardly any Hindu who does not regard the Vedas as the most sacred book of his religion. Yet, says Ambedkar, there are several questions that arise in connection with them. What is their origin? Who is their author? What is their authority? What is their moral or spiritual value?

The first is the riddle about the origin of the Vedas. There is hardly any Hindu who can offer a clear and a definite answer to this simple question. Ambedkar states that so many different but vague answers have been given by the Hindus to this simple question. One answer given by the Hindus about the origin of the Vedas is that they are Sanatana which means they are 'eternally pre-existing' (BAWS 4: 17). Another explanation of the origin of the Vedas is attributed to Prajapati, that is, the Vedas were produced by Agni (fire), Vayu (wind), and Surya (the sun). Further, the legends regarding the origin of the Vedas are also to be found in the Upanishads. The Smritis and Puranas also have to say about the origin of the Vedas. Some say that the Vedas are reproduced from memory.

Thus, the question is: who made the Vedas? The Vedas could not have come into being *ex-nihilo*. They must have a beginning though they may have no end. Why don't the Brahmins speak openly? Why this circumlocution? Ambedkar writes, "This bewildering multiplicity of answers to a simple question is a riddle. The writers who have come forward to furnish these answers are all Brahmins. They belong to the same Vaidik school of thought. They alone were the guardians of the ancient religious lore. Why should such a coherent body of scholars have given such incoherent and chaotic answers to a very simple question?" (BAWS 4: 24).

The second riddle about the Vedas is: Who is the author of the Vedas? The belief of the Hindu or a Brahmin is that the Vedas are supernatural productions; or to use the technical term, the Vedas are *Apaurusheya* i.e. made by a non-human agency.

Ambedkar refutes the above view. He asserts that the Vedas are not supernatural productions; the *Rishis* are the authors of the hymns contained in the Vedas. The Vedas have been treated by the Rishis themselves as human and historical. The hymns of Rig-Veda distinguish between ancient and modern Rishis. Ambedkar, therefore, states, 'Given this abundance of evidence to prove the human origin of the Vedas it is a riddle to find that the Brahmins should so strenuously propagate so extravagant view that the Vedas are of supernatural origin. What made the Brahmins propagate such a view?" (BAWS 4 : 31).

The third riddle of the Vedas, according to Ambedkar is: What is the authority of the Vedas? With regard to this, he says that there prevail two distinct dogmas amongst the Hindus. The first is that the Vedas are 'eternal'. The second dogma is that the Vedas are not only sacred but they are also 'infallible'. Ambedkar rejects both these dogmas and calls them 'absurd'. He states that 'given that the Rishis are the authors of the Vedas the dogma as to their eternal character is an absurdity' (BAWS 4: 136). He writes, "The riddle is why did the Brahmins propound this doctrine of the eternity of the Vedas? Why did the Brahmins adopt such an absurd reasoning in support of their doctrine ?" (BAWS 4: 140).

Further, the second dogma that Vedas are 'infallible' is also 'absurd' in Ambedkar's view. Given the nature and substance of the contents of the Vedas, Ambedkar is amazed, and writes, "Why the Brahmins claimed infallibility for such superstitious writings as the *Vedas Vedas*?" To quote him,

> "The Brahmins have propounded a most mischievous dogma and have spread it among the masses. It is the dogma of the infallibility of the Vedas. If the Hindu intellect has ceased to grow and if the Hindu civilisation and culture has become a stagnant and stinking pool, this dogma must be destroyed root and branch if India is to progress. The Vedas are a worthless set of books. There is no reason either to call them sacred or infallible. The Brahmins have invested it with sanctity and infallibility only because by a later interpolation of what is called the Purusha Sukta, the Vedas have made them the lords of the Earth. Nobody has had the courage to ask why these worthless books which contain nothing but invocation to tribal Gods to destroy the Enemies, loot their property and give it to their followers (have been made sacred and infallible). But the time has come when the Hindu mind must be freed from the hold which the silly ideas propagated by the Brahmins, have on them. Without this liberation, India has no future" (BAWS 4: 8-9).

The fourth riddle of the Vedas, according to Ambedkar, is about their contents; have the Vedas any moral or spiritual value? Ambedkar, on the basis of evidences examined by him, denies any spiritual value to the Vedas. He collects the quotations of Charvakas, Brahaspati and the various schools of philosophy such as the Nyaya, Vaishashikha, Purva and Uttar Mimamsa and proves that the Vedas contain the defects of falsehood, self-contradiction and tautology; and that the authors of the Vedas were 'buffoons, knaves and demons' (BAWS 4: 156). Nor does the Rigveda contain elevating examples of moral life. As to philosophy there is nothing of it in the Rigveda. Similarly, he states that Atharva-Veda is nothing but a collection of sorcery, black magic and medicine. He holds that the Vedas may be useful as a source of information regarding the social life of the Aryans. As a picture of primitive life, it is full of curiosity but there is nothing elevating. There are more vices and few virtues. He concludes, 'Enough has been extracted from the Vedas to show that they contain nothing that can be said to be spiritually or morally elevating. Neither the subject-matter nor contents of the Vedas justify the infallibility with which they have been invested. Why then the Brahmins struggle so hard to clothe them with sanctity and infallibility?" (BAWS 4: 452).

Through all the riddles Ambedkar mocks and points out various and extreme inconsistencies in Hinduism and particularly in the Vedas and later Vedic literature. He shows how things have changed at various intervals.

Perhaps most significant critique of Hinduism by Ambedkar is his text *Annihilation of Caste* published in 1936.[3] The text summarizes the argument of his critiques of Hinduism and particularly its caste system. Briefly, it offers the following arguments. The Caste System is not merely a division of labour but a division of labourers. It is a hierarchy in which the divisions of labourers are graded one above the other. It does not allow Hindus to take up occupations where they are wanted, if they do not belong to them by heredity. Further, the caste system is not a division based on choice. Individual sentiment, individual preference, has no place in it. It is based on the dogma of predestination. Caste cannot also maintain a nonexistent 'racial purity'. As a matter of fact, the Caste system came into being long after the different races of India had commingled in blood and culture. It does not demarcate racial division and it is a social division of people of the same race. Besides, it prevents Hindus from forming a real society or nation. He notes that the first and foremost thing that must be recognized is that the Hindu Society is a myth. The name Hindu is itself a foreign name. It was given by the Mohammedans to the natives for the purpose of distinguishing themselves [from them]. He argues that there is an utter lack among the Hindus of what sociologists call 'consciousness of kind'. There is no 'Hindu consciousness of kind'. The consciousness presents in every Hindu is the consciousness of his caste. Further, the Caste System prevents common activity; and by preventing common activity, it has prevented the Hindus from becoming a society with a unified life and a consciousness of its own being. The most problematic feature of the Caste System is its anti-social spirit. In their isolation from one another, these various castes are as much marked by this antisocial spirit, i.e. protecting their own interests. The caste system also undermines the uplift and incorporation of the aboriginal tribes. Further, the higher castes have conspired to keep the lower castes down. On the other hand, caste prevents Hinduism from being a missionary religion. It also deprives Hindus of mutual help, trust, and fellow-feeling. Furthermore, it is a powerful tool for preventing any reform. It destroys public spirit, public opinion, and public charity.

He writes that his idea is a society based on Liberty, Equality, and Fraternity. Ambedkar is pessimistic about the internal reforms in Hinduism. In his view, internal reform of the Caste System is virtually impossible. No reformers, and no appeals to reason, have so far succeeded. Thus, the real key to destroying caste is rejection of the Shastras. However, destroying caste would not destroy the true principles of religion. He observes that a true priesthood should be based on qualification, not heredity. And finally, if Hindu society is to progress, its traditions must be able to evolve. He finally notes, 'The struggle is yours; I have now decided to leave the Hindu fold.'

Ambedkar's critique of Hinduism is no doubt very harassed. Is there nothing positive in Hinduism for him? What is Hinduism's contribution to the world? He points out that Hindu religious and philosophical thought gave rise to an idea which had broader potentialities for producing social democracy than the idea of fraternity. In his view, 'It is the doctrine of Brahmaism' (BAWS 4: 283-85) . He borrowed this word from Prof. Hopkin's *The Epics of India* (BAWS 4: 283-85). What is this Brahmaism?

He notes, it is something novel even to Hindus. Although, the Hindus are familiar with Vedanta and Brahmanism, they are certainly not familiar with 'Brahmaism'. He offers a few words of explanation of it before describing it.

Hinduism consists of three strands of philosophical and religious thought: (1) Brahmaism, (2) Vedanta, and (3) Brahmanism. In his view, although they are correlated, they stand for three different and distinct ideologies.

Getting references from the Upanishads, he notes that the essence of Brahmaism is summed up in a dogma which is stated in three different forms. They are:

(i) *Sarvam Khalvidam Brahma*—All this is Brahma.
(ii) *Aham Brahmasmi*—Atmana (Self) is the same as Brahma. Therefore I am Brahma.
(iii) *Tattvamasi*—Atmana (Self) is the same as Brahma. Therefore thou art also Brahma.

They are called Mahavakyas which means Great Sayings and they sum up the essence of Brahmanism.

On the other, in his view, the following are the dogmas which sum up the teachings of Vedants:

I. Brahma is the only reality.
II. The world is *maya* or unreal.
III. *Jiva* and *Brahma* are—

(i) according to one school, identical;
(ii) according to another, not identical but are elements of him and not separate from him;
(iii) according to the third school, they are distinct and separate.

While, for him, the creed of *Bramhanism* may be summed up in the following dogmas:

(i) Belief in the *chaturvarna*.
(ii) Sanctity and infallibility of the Vedas.
(iii) Sacrifices to Gods the only way to salvation.

He mentions that most people know the distinction between Vedanta and Brahmanism and the points of controversy between them, but very few people know the distinction between Brahmaism and Vedanta. Even Hindus are not aware of the doctrine of Brahmaism and the distinction between it and Vedanta (BAWS 4: 284). In his view, the distinction is obvious. While Brahmaism and Vedanta agree that Atman is the same as Brahma, the two differ in that Brahmaism does not treat the world as unreal, while Vedanta does. This is the fundamental difference between the two.

The essence of Brahmaism is that the world is real and the reality behind the world is *Brahma*. Everything, therefore, is of the essence of Brahma (BAWS 4: 284).

Having discussed it, he then proceeds to defend the two criticisms which have been levelled against Brahmaism. He notes that it is said that Brahmaism is a piece of impudence. For a man to say "I am *Brahma*" is a kind of arrogance. The other criticism levelled against Brahmaism is the inability of man to know *Brahma*. The phrase 'I am *Brahma*', he argues, may appear impudent. But it can also be an assertion of one's own worth. In a world where humanity suffers so much from an inferiority complex such an assertion on the part of man is to be welcomed (BAWS 4: 284). Democracy demands that each individual shall have every opportunity for realizing his or her worth. It also requires that each individual knows that he is as good as everybody else. Further, those who sneer at *Aham Brahmasmi* (I am *Brahma*) as an impudent utterance forget the other part of the *Maha Vakya* namely *Tatvamasi* (Thou art also Brahma). If *Aham Brahmasmi* had stood alone without the conjunct of *Tatvamasi* it may not have been possible to sneer at it. But with the conjunct of *Tatvamasi* the charge of selfish arrogance cannot stand against Brahmaism, (BAWS 4: 284). It may well be that *Brahma* is unknowable. But all the same this theory of *Brahma* has certain social implications which have tremendous value as a foundation for democracy.

NOTES

1. Dr. B.R. Ambedkar's tract "Philosophy of Hinduism" is part of the third volume of *Dr. Babasaheb Ambedkar: Writings and Speeches* published by the Education Department of the Government of Maharashtra in 1987. The text is available both in electronic and hard copy form. The editor of the vol. 3 notes that 'This script on Philosophy of Hinduism was found as a well-bound copy which we feel is complete by itself. The whole script seems to be a Chapter of one big scheme. This foolscap original typed copy consists of 169 pages' (BAWS 3: 1). It also notes, this particular work 'Philosophy of Hinduism' is 'significant and unique in several aspects'. Firstly, the contents of this work were hitherto unknown. These are the unpublished writings of Dr. Ambedkar which were in the custody of the Administrator General and the custodian of Dr. Ambedkar's property.... These writings had assumed such significance that it was even feared that they had been destroyed or lost. There is a second reason why this work is significant... his interpretation of the philosophy and his historical analysis of the Hindu religion... throws new light on his critique of religious thought. The third important point is that his analysis of

Hindu Philosophy "...(is) a definite approach to the strengthening of ... the solidarity of Indian society based on the human values of equality, liberty, and fraternity. The analysis ultimately points towards uplifting the down-trodden and absorbing masses in the national mainstream" (BAWS 3: 1).

2. 'Riddles in Hinduism' is one of Ambedkar's many works that did not get printed during his lifetime. He started writing this book in the first week of January 1954 and completed it by the end of November 1955. When this book was published by the Government of Maharashtra in 1987, the Shiv Sena sought a ban, but it was published under BAWS Volume 4 and featured twenty-four riddles and eight appendices. The genre of this text is Politics, Society, Religion, and Spirituality.
3. In a letter dated 12 December, 1935, the secretary of the Jat-Pat Todak Mandal (Society for the Abolition of the Caste System), an anti-caste Hindu reformist group organisation based at Lahore, invited B.R. Ambedkar to deliver a speech on the caste system in India at their annual conference in 1936. Ambedkar wrote the speech as an essay under the title 'Annihilation of Caste' and sent it in advance to the organizers in Lahore for printing and distribution. Some of the content was deemed 'objectionable' by the organizers. Therefore, they sought the deletion of sections of the more controversial content endangering Brahminical interests. They wrote to Ambedkar seeking the removal of sections which they found, in their words, 'unbearable'. Ambedkar declared in response that he 'would not change a comma' in his text. After much deliberation, the committee of organizers decided to cancel their annual conference in its entirety. They feared violence by orthodox Hindus at the venue. Ambedkar subsequently published 1500 copies of the speech as a book on 15 May, 1936 at his own expense.

REFERENCE

Babasaheb Ambedker: Writings and Speeches (BAWS), Vol. 1, 3, 4. New Delhi: Dr. Ambedkar Foundation, Ministry of Social Justice & Empowerment, Government of India.

6
Savarkar's *The Essentials of Hindutva*

Hindutva is not a word but a history

(Savarkar, 1969: 3)

Through Chapter three, we saw how Savarkar's Hindutva originated and developed over time. Our investigation was based on his biographical narratives as well as other studies and sources related to the theme. Now, the focus of this chapter will primarily be on Hindutva, which is his key principle. For the purposes of this discussion, we will focus on his text *Essentials of Hindutva* (1923).[1] The text attempts to define and construct the notions of Hindu, Hinduism, and particularly Hindutva. In Hindu nationalist and Hindutva literature, it has taken the place of the Classics, and it is still a key philosophical basis for those who believe in Hindu Rashtra. In addition to this text, we will also examine the arguments of Savarkar's *Hindu Rashtra Darshan* in this chapter. This is the compilation of six of his presidential addresses to the Hindu Mahasabha from 1937 to 1942.

The central aim of his book is to answer the question "Who is a Hindu".[2] He writes, "To this category of names which have been to mankind a subtle source of life and inspiration belongs the word Hindutva, the essential nature and significance of which we have to investigate into" (Savarkar, 1969: 3). The difficulty with defining Hindutva is that as Savarkar points out the ideas and ideals, the systems and societies, the thoughts and sentiments which have centred around this name are so varied and rich, so powerful and so subtle, so elusive and yet so vivid that the term Hindutva defies all attempts at analysis. Thus, he claims that 'Hindutva is not a word but a history' (*ibid.*, 3). This history is not only the spiritual or religious history but a 'history in full'. Significantly, he makes a distinction between Hindutva and Hinduism. 'Hinduism is only a derivative, a fraction, a part of Hindutva' (*ibid.*, 3).

Making it little more clear, he argues, "By an 'ism' it is generally meant a theory or a code more or less based on spiritual or religious dogma or creed. Had not linguistic usage stood in our way then 'Hinduness' would have certainly been a better word than Hinduism as a near parallel to Hindutva. Hindutva embraces all the departments of thought and activity of the whole Being of our Hindu race" (*ibid.*, 4). Savarkar emphasizes that Hinduism represents dogmas or creeds, while Hindutva does not. He writes that he is not attempting a definition of the more limited term Hinduism, which has dogma and creed, but his project is to understand Hindu to understand Hindutva.

Savarkar finds it difficult to define who is Hindu? The reason is failure to distinguish between these two terms—Hinduism and Hindutva. It has also resulted in 'misunderstanding and mutual suspicion' between some of those sister communities that have inherited this 'inestimable and common treasure of our Hindu civilization' (*ibid.*, 3).

He, in the sub-section of this text, 'what is a Hindu?' describes the historical view on the term Hindu. He claims that it is based on 'solid recorded facts'. In his view, 'We don't know exactly when the first intrepid Aryans made it to the Sindhu, the Indus River, but it was before the Egyptians and Babylonians'. He further notes, "By the time the Aryans got to Indus, they had developed a sense of nationality and given it a name, 'Sapta Sindhus'. The Rigveda records this as applying to all of Vedic India. Describing it, he mentions, Sindhu is a variation on Indus River and the S and H being interchanged in Sanskrit, Sindhu indicates Hindu. Savarkar also claims that other nations also recognized the Hindus. The Persians designated Vedic Aryans as Hindus. Local tribes, who contacted the Persians, must have also known the Aryans as Hindus. Later in the text Savarkar argues "it is quite probable that the great Indus was known as Hindu to the original inhabitants of our land and owing to vocal peculiarity of the Aryans it got changed into Sindhu when they adopted it by the operation of the same rule that S is the Sanskritised equivalent of H. Thus Hindu would be the name that this land and the people that inhabited it bore from time so immemorial that even the Vedic name Sindhu is but a later and secondary form of it" (*ibid.*, 10). Thus, he insists that the term Hindu goes back to the beginning of mythology or even the culture of antiquity.

Savarkar then proceeds on to describe Hindu as a nation. The activities of so intrepid a people as the Sindhus or Hindus could no longer be kept cooped or cabined within the narrow compass of the Panchanad or the Punjab. Thus, the Hindus spread "led by the consciousness of a great mission and their Sacrificial Fire that was the symbol thereof" (*ibid*., 10) and 'they soon reclaimed the vast, waste and but very thinly populated lands. Forests were felled, agriculture flourished, cities rose, kingdoms thrived—the touch of the human hand changed the whole face of the wild and unkemp nature'(*ibid*., 11).

Elaborating further, he argues that cities arose and kingdoms thrived. But due to the Aryans' individualistic tendencies, their policies were loosely centralized. As their reach increased, they brought other highly developed folks into their orbit. Keeping distant from locals, they adopted new names such as Kurus, Kashis, and Magadhas, while the old generic term of Sindhus or Hindus was largely forgotten. Thus, not that the concept of national and cultural unity vanished, it just took other names. This growth peaked when 'the valorous Prince of Ayodhya made a triumphant entry in Ceylon and actually brought the whole land from the Himalayas to the Seas under one sovereign sway' (*ibid*., 11).

In his text, Savarkar gives a poetic description of how the event of the home coming of Ramchandra to Ayodhya was 'the real birth-day of our Hindu people' and 'truly our national day'. In his words, "The day when the Horse of Victory returned to Ayodhya unchallenged and unchallengeable, the great white Umbrella of Sovereignty was unfurled over that Imperial throne of Ramchandra, the brave, Ramchandra the good, and a loving allegiance to him was sworn, not only by the Princes of Aryan blood but Hanuman, Sugriva, Vibhishana from the south—that day was the real birth-day of our Hindu people. It was truly our national day: for Aryans and Anaryans knitting themselves into a people were born as a nation. It summed up and politically crowned the efforts of all the generations that preceded it and it handed down a new and common mission, a common banner, a common cause which all the generations after it had consciously or unconsciously fought and died to defend" (*ibid*., 11-12).

He further provides historical proof of Indian antiquity in a sub-section titled 'other name'. He argues that the terms 'Aryavarta' or 'Bramhavarta' were not so suitable as to express the vast synthesis that embraced the whole continent from the Indus to the sea. The objective of this synthesis was to unite them as one nation. Although 'Aryavarta' was best suited to the circumstances which gave it birth, however it could not serve as a common name to a people that had welded Aryans and non-Aryans into a common race and had carried their culture-empire far beyond the bending summits of 'Vindhyadri'. Thus, a suitable alternative name was found to indicate the Indian Nation 'when the House of Bharat came to exercise its sway over the entire world' (*ibid*., 13). He argues that there is no need to debate whether he was Vedic or a Jain or the exact dates of his rule. Subordinate groups took up the term 'Bharatkhanda'. Savarkar claimes that 'Bharatkhanda' indicates "politically grander" from the Himalayas to the sea, as well as "a common cultural empire" (*ibid*., 13). He quotes Vishnu Puran arguing that we have met with no better attempt to define our position as a people than the terse two-line couplet in the Vishu Puran, "The land which is to the north of the sea and to the south of the Himalaya mountain is named Bharata inhabited by the descendants of are Bharata" (*ibid*., 13).

However, the name Bharata did not totally suppress the name Hindu or Sindhu. It is apparent that the epithet Bharatakhand almost succeeded in overshadowing the cradle name of our nation in India. The foreign nations seem to have cared little for it and as our frontier provinces continued to be known by their ancient name, so even our immediate neighbours—the Avestic Persians, the Jews, the Greeks and others clung to our ancient name Sindhus or Hindus. They did not merely indicate the borderland of Indus but the whole nation. The Jews and Greeks continued to call us Sindhus or Hindus. Even Huen-tsang, Savarkar writes, who lived so long with us persists in calling us Shintus or Hintus. Down to this day, he further mentions, the whole world knows us as 'Hindus' and our land as 'Hindustan'. This is in fulfilment of the wishes of our Vedic fathers who were the first to make that choice.

Savarkar notes that names are for others, more than for ourselves. In his words, "This fact added to the circumstances which brought us first into contact and then into a fierce conflict with the world at large, soon enabled the epithet Hindu to assert itself once more and so vigorously as to push into the background even the well beloved name of Bharatakhanda itself" (*ibid*., 16).

Asserting and reflecting on the name Bharatkhand, Savarkar then turns to international acceptance of the name. In his view, Hindusthan was by no means cut off from the world when Buddhism emerged. At that time, Hindusthan had filled up its land, and India had become the heart and soul of almost the whole then known world. The outsiders who poured in to learn and trade came to call us Hindus too. Buddhism helped the name to grow in prominence throughout the world and made us more conscious of ourselves as Hindus.

Savarkar raises certain questions about the fall of Buddhism. 'Can it be that philosophical differences alone could have made our nation turn against Buddhism?' 'Can it be the inanitation and demoralization of the

Buddhistic Church itself?' (*ibid.*, 18). "Not wholly", he observes, and tells that such shortcomings "would not have attracted such fierce attention and proved fatal to Buddhistic power in India had not the political consequences of the Buddhistic expansion been so disastrous to the national virility and even the national existence of our race" (*ibid.*, 18). He asserts that the Buddhist faith made people too passive and thus facilitated the Huns taking over India. But Hindus "could not drink with equanimity this cup of bitterness and political servitude at the hands of those whose barbarous violence could still be soothed by the mealy-mouthed formulas of *Ahimsa* and spiritual brotherhood" (*ibid.*, 19). He does not mean to rebuke Buddhism, "We yield to none in our love, admiration and respect for the Buddha—the Dharma—the Sangha. They are all ours. Their glories are ours and ours their failures" (*ibid.*, 20). But, even holier things preceded the Buddhists, Hindu statesmen that allowed Buddhism to become what it became. 'So, we do not think that the political virility or the manly nobility of our race began and ended with the Mauryas alone—or was a consequence of their embracing Buddhism. But Hindus could not be other worldly while dominated by Huns whose whole creed could be summed in two words, "Fire and Sword" (*ibid.*, 21). And Buddhism had no 'logic and no argument' that could counter the 'Fire and Sword' doctrine. 'So the leaders of thought and action of our race had to rekindle their Sacrificial Fire to oppose the sacrilegious one and to re-open the Vedic fields for steel, to get it sharpened on the 'altar of Kali' (*ibid.*, 21). The Hindus drove the invaders back to Tartary and Mongolia. On the other hand, "Back to the Vedas! The national cry grew louder and louder, more and more imperative, because this was essentially a political necessity" (*ibid.*, 22).

Despite this, Savarkar praises Buddhism. One of the subtitles of his text is '*Buddhism—A universal religion*'. He writes, "Buddhism had made the first and yet the greatest attempt to propagate a universal religion. Go, ye Bhikkus, to all the ten directions of the world and preach the law of Righteousness! Truly, it was a law of Righteousness. It had no ulterior end in view, no lust for land or lucre quickening its steps; but grand though its achievements were it could not eradicate the seeds of animal passions nor of political ambitions nor of individual aggrandizement in the minds of all men to such an extent as to make it safe for India to change her sword for a rosary" (*ibid.*, 22).

Yet, he argues that grand though its achievements were, Buddhism 'could not eradicate the seeds of animal passions nor of political ambitions nor of individual aggrandizement'. India did try to incorporate and live up to Buddhist precepts to the best of its ability. "Nobly did she try to kill killing by getting killed—and at last found out that palm leaves at times are too fragile for steel!" (*ibid*., 23). Further, "the leaders of thought and action grew sick of repeating the mumbos and jumbos of universal brotherhood" (*ibid*., 23).

'Then came reaction', Savarkar writes, "The reaction against universal tendencies of Buddhism only grew more insistent and powerful as the attempt to re-establish the Buddhist power in India began to assume a more threatening attitude" (*ibid*., 25). We were aware of people in our ranks who sympathized with the enemy. Buddhist armies, stationed in China readied for attack but they lost. And, "They had to formally renounce all ulterior national aims against India and give a pledge that they would never again enter India with any political end in view" (*ibid*., 26). Savarkar quotes *Bhavishya-Purana, Pratisarga-Parva* and writes, "All the Buddhists swore there and then that they would not come to the Aryadesh with any territorial designs". However, in his view, "The Buddhists as individuals had nothing to fear from India, the land of toleration, but they should give up all dreams of endangering the national life of India and her independence" (*ibid*., 26).

His text then informs us that as a part of this 'retrenching' in the face of the Buddhist, some institutions were revived. One of such institutions was the system of 'four varnas' which became popular. He argues, "From this it was a natural step to prohibit our people from visiting shores which were uncongenial—in some cases fiercely hostile—to such peculiar institutions" (*ibid*., 27). Conversely, the nation developed a stronger sense of self-knowledge in order to fight off the Buddhists. But, in our North-Western borders, there was a comingling of races that were 'growing rather too unceremoniously to be healthy and our frontiers too shift to be safe'. Thus, a boundary was drawn. And it was the Sindhu River.

Savarkar again quotes *Bhavishya Puran*, *Pratisarga-Parva* and mentions that the best country of the Aryans is known as Sindhusthan, whereas the Mlecch Country lies beyond the Indus. This demarcation was made by the great king, Shalivahan the grandson of the great Vikramaditya. Thus, "The day on which the patriarchs of our race crossed that stream they ceased to belong to the people they had left behind and laid the foundation of a new nation" (*ibid*., 30). They assimilated and expanded and created 'a race and a new polity that could only be most fittingly and feelingly described as Sindhu or Hindu'.

He, then, highlights the advantage of the term Sindhustan. He mentions that Bharatvarsha is, and must be a latter designation besides being personal in its appeal. It refers to a particular King. Emperor Bharat is gone, but Sindhu goes on for ever. In his words, "It is the vital spinal cord that connects the remotest past to the remotest future" (*ibid.*, 31). This must be why the leaders must have restored the 'ancient Vedic name of our land and nation Sindusthan—the best nation of Aryans'. Another advantage to the name is that 'Sindhu in Sanskrit does not only mean the Indus, but also the Sea—which girdles the Southern peninsula'. Savarkar points to the geographical significance of the terms and notes, 'the epithet Sindhusthan calls up the image of our whole Motherland; the land that lies between Sindhu and Sindhu—from the Indus to the Seas'.

Yet, in his formulation, Sindhustan does not only refer to geography. In his view, the concept expressed by this word was 'national' and not merely 'geographical'. "Sindhusthan was not merely a piece of land but it was a nation which was ideally if not always actually a state (rajnah-rashtram)" (*ibid.*, 32). Further, Sindhusthan refers to the culture. Sindusthan was the 'Best nation of the Aryas'. Elaborating it, he notes, the term 'is not based on any theological hair-splitting or fanaticism'. The word Arya expressly refers to all who have inherited a common culture, common blood, common country and common polity. While word Mlechcha was in opposition to Sindhustan which meant foreigners nationally and racially, and not necessarily religiously.

The main source of Savarkar's depiction of Indian history are early Hindu texts, especially Puranas and epics. He writes that we owe a debt of gratitude to these Puranas and Epics for having preserved all ancient and venerable records of our people through revolutions which had effaced the very traces of whole nations and whole civilizations elsewhere in the world. In his view, these records of ancient and patriotic Puranas and Histories (*Itihasas*) are 'more faithful, accurate, and reliable' than the modern updated 'western puranas'. He sarcastically remarks that western modern puranas have such convincing discoveries to their credit "as the one which assures us that *Ramayana* sings of the foundation of Vijayanagar or the other which asserts that Gautam the Buddha was merely the Sun or the Dawn personified !"

He, then, turns to the issue of language and the politics of naming. On this point, he argues that the rise and fall of Buddhism were accompanied by a remarkable spread and growth of the vernacular. On the other hand, Sanskrit got confined in a classical fortress. 'Prakrit' (Hindi) became the living thoughts of the people. While Sanskrit writers generally preferred the word 'Bharat', as it was more in consonance with the established canons of elegance, 'Hindusthan' stuck in popular and living culture. Further, while Sanskrit was the linguistic and cultural backbone,

Prakrit (Hindi), an elder daughter of Sanskrit, became the living spoken tongue. Centuries prior to the British, Savarkar argues, Hindi or Hindustani was the mother tongue for those crossing the nation. He offers several arguments in its favour:

> "Hindusthani is par excellence the language of Hindusthan or Sindhusthan. The attempt to raise Hindi to the pedestal of our national tongue is neither new nor forced. Centuries before the advent of British rule in India we find it recorded in our annals that this was the medium of expression throughout India. A *sadhu* or a merchant starting from Rameshwaram and proceeding to Hardwar, could make himself understood in all parts of India through this tongue. Sanskrit might have introduced him to circles of *pandits* and princes; but Hindusthani was a safe and sure passport to the Rajasabhas as well as to the bazaars. A Nanak, a Chaitanya, a Ramdas could and did travel up and down the country as freely as they would have done in their own provinces teaching and preaching in this tongue. As the growth and development of this our genuine national tongue was parallel to and almost simultaneous with the revival and popularization of the ancient names Sindhusthan or Sindhus or Hindusthan or Hindus it was but a matter of course that language being the common possession of the whole nation should be called Hindusthani or Hindi" (*ibid.*, 41).

Savarkar, then, turns to the relationship between 'national language' and 'political unity'. "From Ceylon to Kashmir the Rajputs—a single family of princes—ruled, often connected closely by marriages and more closely by the tradition of chivalry and culture handed down by common law. The whole life of the nation was being brought into a harmony as rich as divine, and the growth of the national language was but an outward expression of this inward unity of our national life" (*ibid.*, 42).

Savarkar, then, comes to foreign invaders. He notes, "The Mohammedans had crossed that stream even under Kasim, but it was a wound only skin-deep, for the heart of our people was not hurt and was not even aimed at. The contest began in grim earnestness with Mohammad and ended, shall we say, with Abdalli ? From year to year, decade to decade, century to century, the contest continued. Arabia ceased to be what Arabia was; Iran annihilated; Egypt, Syria, Afghanistan, Baluchistan, Tartary,—from Granada to Gazni—nations and civilizations fell in heaps before the sword of Islam of Peace!! But here for the first time the sword succeeded in striking but not in killing" ...The contrast was not only grim but it was monstrously unequal. It was not a race, a nation or a people India had to struggle with. It was nearly all Asia, quickly to be followed by nearly all Europe. ...Day after day, decade after decade, century after century, the ghastly conflict continued and India single-handed kept up the fight morally and militarily. The moral victory was won when Akbar came to the throne and Darashukoh was born" (*ibid.*, 44).

This is the context in which Savarkar presents his viewpoints on 'Hindutva at work'. He writes that during this prolonged furious conflict, the Hindus became more aware of themselves and glued together as a nation in a way never seen before. There was no divide between sects. "It must not be forgotten that we have all along referred to the progress of the Hindu movement as a whole and not to that of any particular creed or religious section thereof—of Hindutva and not Hinduism only. Sanatanists, Satnamis, Sikhs, Aryas, Anaryas, Marathas and Madrasis, Brahmins and Panchamas—all suffered as Hindus and triumphed as Hindus. Both friends and foes contributed equally to enable the words Hindu and Hindusthan to supersede all other designations of our land and our people" (*ibid.*, 45).

Further, "All those on this side of the Indus who claimed the land from Sindhu to Sindhu, from the Indus to the seas, as the land of their birth, felt that they were directly mentioned by that one single expression, Hindusthan. The enemies hated us as Hindus and the whole family of peoples and races, of sects and creeds that flourished from Attock to Cuttack was suddenly individualised into a single Being" (*ibid.*, 45).

What we note from the above discussion is that the idea of Hindu unity is seen in relation to the 'other' or 'outsider'. It is the 'we' versus 'them' which is at work here. It is this binary in which Savarkar locates his idea of Hindutva.

Thus, he argues, Hindutva refers to all as a unit who suffered under the invaders. Hindutva was the ideology of those who fought. "This one word, *Hindutva*, ran like a vital spinal cord through our whole body politic and made the Nayars of Malabar weep over the sufferings of the Brahmins of Kashmir. Our bards bewailed the fall of Hindus, our seers roused the feelings of Hindus, our heroes fought the battles of Hindus, our saints blessed the efforts of Hindus, our statesmen moulded the fate of Hindus, our mothers wept over the wounds and gloried over the triumphs of Hindus" (*ibid.*, 46).

He mentions that it will take volumes to note all the testimonials to those who cultivated and fought in the name of Hindutva. However, he offers some examples in his text to prove his point. After setting different examples, and making analysis of the history of Hindu and Hindusthan, he in the subtitle 'stupid notion must go' writes, "having thus tried to trace the successive chapters of the history of the words Hindu and Hindusthan from the earliest Vedic period to the fall of the last of our Hindu empire in 1818 A.D., we are now in a position to address ourselves to the main task of determining the essentials of Hindutva" (*ibid.*, 70).

In his book, we see that Savarkar traces the history of the words Hindu and Hindusthan almost until the halfway mark. He provides several arguments to support his views and refutes other prevalent notions in regard to the word Hindu and Hindusthan. He, then, mentions, "The first result of this enquiry is to explode the baseless suspicion which has crept into the minds of some of our well-meaning but hasty countrymen that the origin of the words Hindu and Hindusthan is to be traced to the malice of the Mohammedans!" (*ibid.*, 70-71).

In his view, "Long before Mohammad was born, nay, long before the Arabians were heard of as a people, this ancient nation was known to ourselves as well as to the foreign world by the proud epithet Sindhu or Hindu and Arabians could not have invented this term, any more than they could have invented the Indus itself" (*ibid.*, 71).

He, then, makes his own position: "Now we are fairly in a position to try to analyse the contents of one of the most comprehensive and bewilderingly synthetic concept known to human tongue. Hindutva is a derivative word from Hindu, we have seen that the earliest and the most sacred records of our race show that the appellation, Saptasindhu or Hapt-Hindu was applied to a region in which the Vedic nation flourished. The geographical sense being the primary one has, now contracting, now expanding, but always persistently been associated with the words Hindu and Hindus than till after the lapse of nearly 5000 years if not more, Hindusthan has come to mean the whole continental country from the Sindhu to Sindhu from the Indus to the Seas"(*ibid.*, 81-82). He, further, observes, "The most important factor that contributes to the cohesion, strength and the sense of unity of a people is that they should possess an internally well-connected and externally well-demarcated local habitation, and a 'name' that could, by its very mention, rouse the cherished image of their motherland as well as the loved memories of their past" (*ibid.*, 82).

He praises the motherland as follows, "We are happily blessed with both these important requisites for a strong and united nation. Our land is so vast and yet so well-knit, so well demarcated from others and yet so strongly entrenched that no country in the world is more closely marked out by the fingers of nature as a geographical unit beyond cavil or criticism, as also is the name Hindusthan or Hindu that it has come to bear" (*ibid*., 82). The first image, he mentions, is of motherland. Hindusthan means the land of Hindus, so 'the first essential of Hindutva' must automatically be this geographical element. A Hindu, in his view, is 'primarily a citizen either in himself or through his forefathers of 'Hindusthan' and who claims the land as his motherland" (*ibid*., 82).

In the subtitle 'Essential implications of Hindutva', he points out his essentials of Hindutva. He writes, "We must try, therefore, to be on our guard so that in our attempt to determine the essentials of Hindutva we be guided entirely by the actual contents of the word as it stands at present" (*ibid*., 83). It is here that Savarkar makes a difference between Hindu and Indian. He fears, "although the root-meaning of the word Hindu like the sister epithet Hindi may mean only an Indian, yet as it is we would be straining the usage of words too much—we fear, to the point of breaking—if we call a Mohammedan a Hindu because of his being a resident of India" (*ibid*., 83).

It is possible that at some future time, he argues, the word Hindu may simply refer to a citizen of Hindustan and nothing else. However, it is possible only if every other 'ism' is disowned and they have adopted our culture and our history, inherited our blood, and come to see our land not only as the land of their love but even the land of their worship. Thus, in Savarkar's view "the first requisite of Hindutva is that he be a citizen of Hindusthan either by himself or through his forefathers, yet it is not the only requisite qualification of it, as the term Hindu has come to mean much more than its geographical significance" (*ibid*., 84).

He makes another criterion to determine who should be called a Hindu. He argues that Hindu cannot be synonymous with Bharatiya or Hindi. "The reason that explains why the term Hindu cannot be synonymous with Bharatiya or Hindi and mean an Indian only, naturally introduces us to the second essential implication of that term. The Hindus are not merely the citizens of the Indian state because they are united not only by the bonds of the love they bear to a common motherland but also by the bonds of a common blood. They are not only a Nation but also a race—jati" (*ibid*., 84).

The word jati derived from the root Jan to produce, means a brotherhood, a race determined by a common origin, possessing a common blood. All Hindus claim to have in their veins the blood of the mighty race incorporated with and descended from the Vedic fathers, the Sindhus. Here his position cannot be seen only in relation to the moslems.

He was really responding to the colonial discourse that propagated that India cannot be a nation because it does not belong to one race.

Savarkar writes that we are all well aware of the objection that 'Is your race really a race?' He argues that if English, German, French, Chinese can claim to be a race despite freely incorporating foreign blood into theirs through marriage, then so too can Hindus. As a statement of the racial unity of Hindus, he presents his own interpretation of history. "No word can give full expression to this racial unity of our people as the epithet, Hindu, does. Some of us were Aryans and some Anaryans; but Ayars and Nayars—we were all Hindus and own a common blood. Some of us are Brahmans and some Namashudras or Panchamas; but Brahmans or Chandalas—we are all Hindus and own a common blood...... We feel we are a JATI, a race bound together by the dearest ties of blood and therefore it must be so" (*ibid.*, 89-90).

He further supports his argument by stating that "And speaking relatively alone, no people in the world can more justly claim to get recognized as a racial unit than the Hindus and perhaps the Jews. A Hindu marrying a Hindu may lose his caste but not his Hindutva. A Hindu believing in any theoretical or philosophical or social system, orthodox or heterodox, provided it is unquestionably indigenous and founded by a Hindu may lose his sect but not his Hindutva—his Hinduness—because the most important essential which determines it is the inheritance of the Hindu blood. Therefore, all those who love the land that stretches from Sindhu to Sindhu, from the Indus to the Seas, as their fatherland consequently claim to inherit the blood of the race that has evolved, by incorporation and adaptation, from the ancient Saptasindhus can be said to possess two of the most essential requisites of Hindutva" (*ibid.*, 90).

The third criterion, Savarkar sets to be called Hindu is 'Hindu culture'. He writes, "Hindus are bound together not only by the tie of the love we bear to a common fatherland and by the common blood that courses through our veins and keeps our hearts throbbing and our affections warm, but also by the tie of the common homage we pay to our great civilization—our Hindu culture" (*ibid.*, 91-92). Thus, he concludes, "We are one because we are a nation, a race and own a common Sanskriti (civilization)" (*ibid.*, 92).

By establishing the criteria, he then attempts to illustrate the theme of civilization, which was an overarching theme of the 20th century. In the subtitle of the text 'What is Civilization?', Savarkar elaborates his views. In his definition, 'Civilization is the expression of the mind of man' (*ibid.*,

92). Further, 'Civilization is the account of what man has made of matter'. 'If matter is the creation of the Lord, then civilization is the miniature secondary creation of man'. 'At its best it is the perfect triumph of the soul of man over matter and man alike' (*ibid.*, 92). Tracing this definition of civilization in nation, he writes, "The story of the civilization of a nation is the story of its thoughts, its actions and its achievements. Literature and art tell us of its thoughts; history and social institutions of its actions and achievements" (*ibid.*, 92).

He is convinced that civilizations may borrow much, 'yet their civilization is too characteristic to be mistaken for any other cultural unit'. His text lists cultural items that all Hindus and only Hindus understand. 'We understood our Hindu heroes as people who fought and died for us'. Savarkar also observes that wars among Hindus do not mean that Hindus are divided and separate as a people. He also offers the counter-argument in this context. "But what about the internecine wars amongst Hindus? We answer, what about the Wars of Roses amongst the English? What of the internecine struggle, of state against state, sect against sect, class against class, each invoking foreign help against his own countrymen, in Italy, in Germany, in France, in America? Are they still a people, a nation and do they possess a common history ? If they do, the Hindus do. If the Hindus do not possess a common history, then none in the world does" (*ibid.*, 95).

He further argues that 'our history tells the story of the action of our race, so does our literature taken in its fullest sense tell the story of the thought of our race' and the works of art and architecture are also a common inheritance of our race, whether they be representative of the Vaidik or Avaidik school of thought. He further maintains that common laws and rites among Hindus also prove its basic unity. Common institutions and a common law that sanctions and sanctifies them, however, they may differ in details are nevertheless both the cause and the effect of the basic unity of our race. Again, "We have feasts and festivals in common. We have rites and rituals in common. The Dasara and the Divali the Rakhibandhan and the Holi are welcomed wherever a Hindu breathes, Sikhs and Jains, Brahmans and Panchams alike. You would find the whole Hindu kingdom enfete on the Divali day, not only Hindusthan, but the Greater Hindusthan that is fast growing in all the continents of the world" (*ibid.*, 98).

Savarkar points out that "These then in short—and the subject in hand does not permit us to be exhaustive on this point—constitute the essence of our civilization and mark us out a cultural unit. We Hindus are not only a Rashtra, a *Jati*, but as a consequence of being both, own a common Sanskriti expressed, preserved chiefly and originally through Sanskrit, the real mother tongue of our race. Everyone who is a Hindu inherits this Sanskriti and owes his spiritual being to it as truly as he owes his physical one to the land and the blood of his forefathers" (*ibid.*, 99).

We may note, Savarkar's criterion is exclusive in nature. On the scale of his criterion, the converts to Christianity and Islam are not to be recognized as countrymen, though they have much culturally in common. "Hindusthan to them is Fatherland as to any other Hindu, yet it is not to them a Holy land too. Their holy land is far off in Arabia or Palestine" (*ibid.*, 113). Consequently, their names and their outlook smack of foreign origin. Their love is divided. "They must set their Holy land above their Fatherland in their love and allegiance. That is but natural. We are not condemning nor are we lamenting. We are simply telling facts as they stand" (*ibid.*, 113). He also suggests that reconversion to the Hindu fold is allowed. But those who speak of a distant Holy land cannot be part of Hindutva.

Savarkar, in his text, finally reaches to his definition of who is a Hindu and writes, "A Hindu then is he who feels attachment to the land that extends from Sindhu to Sindhu as the land of his forefathers—as his Fatherland; who inherits the blood of the great race whose first and discernible source could be traced from the Himalayan altitudes of the Vedic Saptasindhus and which assimilating all that was incorporated and ennobling all that was assimilated has grown into and come to be known as the Hindu people; and who, as a consequence of the foregoing attributes, has inherited and claims as his own the Hindu Sanskriti, the Hindu civilization, as represented in a common history, common heroes, a common literature, common art, a common law and a common jurisprudence, common fairs and festivals, rites and rituals, ceremonies and sacraments" (*ibid.*, 100).

Having defined who is a Hindu, and setting the essentials of Hindutva Savarkar defends his thesis. "The limits of this essay do not permit us to determine the nature or the essentials of Hinduism or to try to discuss it at any great length. As we have shown above the enquiry into what is Hinduism can only begin after the question 'who is a Hindu?' is rightly answered determining the essentials of Hindutva ; and as it is only with these essentials of Hindutva, which enable us to know who is a Hindu, that this our present enquiry is concerned, the discussion of Hinduism Falls necessarily outside of our scope"(*ibid.*, 105).

A remarkable aspect of Savarkar's text is his description of Hindu dharma that is found at the end. He observes that the Hindu dharma is 'the conclusion of the conclusions' arrived at by "harmonizing the detailed experience of all the schools of religious thought—Vaidik, Sanatani, Jaini, Bauddh, Sikh or Deva Samaj". "Each one and everyone of those systems or sects which are the direct descendants and developments of the religious beliefs Vaidik and non-Vaidik that obtained in the land of the Saptasindhus or in the other unrecorded communities in other parts of India in the Vedic period, belongs to and is an integral part of Hindu dharma" (*ibid.*, 108). He, briefly, points out his views on Hinduism also. "Hinduism means the system of religious beliefs found common amongst the Hindu people. Hinduism means the "ism" of the Hindu. The word Hindu comes from Sindhu, the Indus. Thus it means the religions that are peculiar and native to this land and these people. You might say these sects contradict each other. But they are all still of the Indus and as such "Hinduism" (*ibid.*, 104).

Savarkar makes a clear difference between 'Hindu dharma' and 'Hindutva'. To quote him, "Hindutva is not identical with Hindu Dharma; nor is Hindu Dharma identical with Hinduism. This twofold mistake that identifies Hindutva with Hindu Dharma and both with Sanatani sect is justly resented by our non-Sanatani sects or religious systems and goads a small section of people amongst them—not to explode this mistaken notion, but unfortunately to commit another grave and suicidal mistake in the opposite direction and disown their Hindutva itself" (*ibid.*, 121).

"This Bharatbhumi, this Sindhusthan, this land of ours that stretches from Sindhu to Sindhu is our *Punyabhumi*, for it was in this land that the Founders of our faith and the Seers to whom 'Veda' the Knowledge was revealed, from Vaidik seers to Dayananda, from Jina to Mahavir, from Buddha to Nagasen, from Nanak to Govind, from Banda to Basava, from Chakradhar to Chaitanya, from Ramdas to Rammohan, our Gurus and Godmen were born and bred. The very dust of its paths echoes the footfalls of our Prophets and Gurus" (*ibid.*, 111). So to every Hindu, from the Santhal to the Sindhu this 'Bharatabhumi' this 'Sindhusthan' is at once a *Pitribhu* and a *Punyabhu*—fatherland and a holy land. After this definition he gives a national call. He writes, "who by race, by blood, by culture, by nationality possess almost all the essentials of Hindutva and had been forcibly snatched out of our ancestral home by the hand of violence—ye, have only to render wholehearted love to our common Mother and recognize her not only as Fatherland (*Pitribhu*) but even as a Holy land (*punyabhu*); and yet would be most welcome to the Hindu fold."

In his last section, he discusses some of the unique natural blessings Hindusthan has received. The central question, he puts in this section is, "we found Hindutva to contribute towards the strength, cohesion, and progress of our people, but is it a ground strong enough to build a future that will repel attacks?" He mentions that some ancient people built huge walls to convert a whole country into a fortified castle. Today their walls are dust. But for Bharat, the Himalayas are Sindhusthan's ramparts, the oceans their moat. "She is the richly endowed, daughter of God—this our Motherland" (*ibid.*, 132). And on and on he writes beautiful poetry about Sindhusthan's natural endowments. And the second essential of Hindusthan (beyond a land) "puts the estimate of our latent powers of national cohesion and greatness yet higher. No country in the world with the exception of China again, is peopled by a race so homogeneous, yet so ancient" (*ibid.*, 132). Muslims and Christians are religious but not a race or national. The Hindus are! "And culture? The English and Americans feel they are kith and kin because they possess Shakespeare in common. The Hindus a *Ramayana* and *Mahabharata* and the *Vedas*. Americans have history of centuries. Hindus in *Kalpas*. "If a people that had no past has no future, then a people that had produced an unending galaxy of heroes . . . [who] fought with and vanquished the forces whose might struck Greece and Rome" (*ibid.*, 134).

Savarkar argues that the notion of Holy land is more powerful than Mother land. He notes, beyond culture, the tie of the common Holy land has often seemed stronger than the bonds of Motherland. In his view, "Muslims would sacrifice all India if that be to the glory of Islam or could save the city of their prophet. Look at the Jews though centuries abroad, they are still super attached to Israel, the land of their Prophets. If a Jewish state ever happens in Palestine, they would naturally set the interests of their Holy land above those of their Motherland in America and Europe. If war happened between their motherland and the Holy land, they'd sympathize with the latter. The crusades again attest to the wonderful influence that a common Holy land exercises over a people widely separated in race, nationality, and language" (*ibid.*, 136).

He creates the 'ideal conditions' for a nation to achieve perfect solidarity and cohesion. This would, other things being equal, be found in the case of those people who inhabit the land they adore, the land of whose forefathers is also the land of their Gods, the scenes of their history and mythology. He argues that only Arabia and Palestine (if it becomes Jewish) have this advantage. But, Arabia is poorer in the natural, cultural, and historical essentials of a great people. And the potential Zionist state too. China alone of the present comity of nations is almost as richly gifted with the geographical, racial, cultural essentials as the Hindus are.

Thus, the actual essentials of Hindutva are the ideal essentials of nationality. In his view, great combinations have become the order of the day. For instance, the League of Nations, Pan-Islamism, Pan-Slavism have developed into greater wholes. He saw these institutions as 'better-fitted for the struggle for 'existence and power'. It is on this basis , he asks for the 'organic unity' of Hindu. He convinces us that whether Jain or Samaji or Sikh or any other sub-section cannot afford to cut themselves off or fall out of the organic combination that already exists. Moreover, in his view, we must strengthen these ties. For this, he prescribes pulling down the barriers that have survived their utility like castes, customs, sects and sections. On the other hand, intermarriages between provinces and provinces, castes and castes, should be encouraged where they do not exist. He warns minorities asking them to remember that they would be cutting the very branch on which they stand, if they did not strengthen every tie that binds them to the main organism, whether of blood or language or common Motherland. Thus, he calls, "Blend blood, from vein to vein, from Attock to Cuttack till at last the Hindu people get fused and welded into an indivisible whole, till our race gets consolidated and strong sharp as steel" (*ibid.*, 139).

> "We are trying our best, as we ought to do, to develop the consciousness of and a sense of attachment to the greater whole, whereby Hindus, Mohammedans, Parsis, Christians and Jews would feel as Indians first and every other thing afterwards. But whatever progress India may have made to that goal one thing remains almost axiomatically true—not only in India but everywhere in the world- that a nation requires a foundation to stand upon and the essence of the life of a nation is the life of that portion of its citizens whose interest and history and aspirations are most closely bound up with the land and who thus provide the real foundation to the structure of their national state" (*ibid.*, 140).

Savarkar notes that Hindus are India's bedrock. Therefore, even from the point of Indian nationality, Hindus must consolidate and strengthen Hindu nationality; not to give wanton offence to any of our non-Hindu compatriots, but in just and urgent defense of our race and land. He observes that as long as competition and pan-movements compete for the world, we must have our team in order. He is optimistic that someday India will be able to dictate claims to the whole earth and they will be in the line of what *Gita* and Buddha lay down. The last passage of his text is as follows, "Thirty crores of people, with India for their basis of operation, for their Fatherland and for their Holy-land with such a history behind them, bound together by ties of a common blood and common culture can dictate their terms to the whole world. A day will come when mankind will have to face the force. Equally certain it is that whenever the Hindu come to hold such a position whence they could dictate terms to the whole world—those terms cannot be very different from the terms which *Gita* dictates' or the Buddha lays down—A Hindu is most intensely so, when he ceases to be Hindu; and with a Shankar claims the whole earth for a Benares 'Waranasi Medini ! 'or with a Tukaram exclaims 'my country ! Oh brothers, 'the limits of the Universe—there the frontiers of my country lie !" (*ibid.*, 141).

Having discussed Savarkar's essentials of Hindutva and his definition of who is Hindu, we turn to his six presidential addresses to the Hindu Mahasabha which have been compiled in the form of the text 'Hindu Rashtra Darshan' . His lectures show some significant features of Hindutva and also his idea of the Hindu nation and Swaraj. Following is an extract from his text 'Hindu Rashtra Darshan' in the context of his idea of Hindutva.

The Swarajaya (he refers to Swaraj as Swarajya in his writings) did not refer only to the political freedom of our country or land, nor to the independence of the geographical unit called India. For him *Swarajaya* was needed as 'Our country is endeared to us because it has been the abode of our race, our people, our dearest and nearest relations and as such is only metaphorically referred to, to express our national being' (Savarkar 2020: 9). Here the idea of race might be underlined. It leads to his Hindu conception of India that he points out, 'Therefore Indian *swarajya* or Indian *swatantrya* means, as far as the Hindu Nation is concerned, the political independence of the Hindus, the freedom which would enable them to grow to their full height' (*ibid.*, 10). He contends that Swarajya must refer to that "Rajya" in which the Hindus' "Swatva" can assert itself without being dominated by any non-Hindu people, be they Indian or extra-Hindu.

For this *Swarajya*, Savarkar emphasizes on language. Thus, his *Swarajya* includes *Sanskritnishtha* Hindi as national language. According to him, 'By Hindi we of course mean the pure '*Sankritnishtha'* Hindi, as we find it for example in the '*Satyartha Prakash'* written by Maharshi Dayanand Saraswati. How simple and unstained with a single unnecessary foreign word is that Hindi and how expressive withal!' (*ibid.*, 47). For him, Sanskrit Nishtha Hindi had nothing to do with the Hindusthani that the Wardha scheme sought to create. Savarkar calls this a 'linguistic monstrosity' that must be ruthlessly suppressed. He is so keen to use this pure Hindi that he observed that it is the bounden duty of Hindus to out ruthlessly all unnecessary alien words whether Arabian or English, from every Hindu tongue. However, showing a utilitarian posture, he mentions that he is not against the English. "We are not against the English or any other language; nay, we insist on the study of the English as an indispensable necessity and a profitable passport to world literature. But we must not allow the influx of alien words into our language without checking their pass and testing their necessity" (*ibid.*, 47).

Hindu Rashtra Darshan also points out his method to attain *Swarajya*. Unlike Gandhi, who employed principled nonviolence for Swaraj, Savarkar saw the use of nonviolence in a very narrow and strategic sense. Moreover, he was open to using violence against the aggression of the British. As far as armed revolt, as a part of his political theory is concerned, in principle he does not reject it. Yet, given the Indian political situation, he does not approve it on strategic grounds. For insistence, during the Second World War, on the possibility of a national armed revolt against the British as British were engaged at war front, he strategically argued that as India was disarmed, disorganized and disunited, thus, an armed revolt against England on a national scale could not be thought. It is important to note that Savarakar's political ethics is utilitarian in nature. To quote him, "the most practical factor and one which ought to be common to all of these schools of moral thought and which alone can practically serve to distinguish a moral act from an immoral one, a virtue from a vice, the good from the bad is the utilitarian principle that everything that contributes under a given set of circumstances to human good is moral, a virtue and the opposite is immoral, a vice under those given circumstances, that all mortality is essentially human" (*ibid.*, 83).

On the basis of this philosophy, he regarded the political theory of absolute non-violence as a crime. As for him, the principle of absolute non-violence and condemning all armed resistance, even against incorrigible aggression, is 'absolutely impracticable, anti-human, and therefore, positively immoral' (*ibid.*, 83). In addition, in his opinion, absolute non-violence, that is non-violence under all circumstances, causes incalculable harm to humanity. While relative non-violence on the whole was doubtless a virtue so pre-eminently 'contributing to human good as to form one of the fundamentals on which human life whether individual or social can take its stand and evolve all social amenities' (*ibid.*, 83). According to him, in the law of nature or in the will of God, there is no room for absolute non-violence. He argues, "man could not have saved himself from utter extinction nor could have but led the precarious and wretched life of a coward and a worm had he not succeeded in adding the strength of artificial Arms to his natural arm" (*ibid.*, 84).

Thus, to him, "The belief in absolute non-violence condemning all armed resistance even to aggression evinces no mahatmaic saintliness but a monomaniacal senselessness" (*ibid.*, 84). On this ground, he noted that Gandhi's political programme based on the monomaniacal principle of absolute non-violence is not worth a moment's consideration. As a pragmatic political theorist, even though on the one hand he rules out an armed rising on a national scale, on the other hand, he criticizes the other extreme of absolute non-violence, which declares all armed resistance as inadmissible and is not only unthinkable but morally unjust.

In Savarkar's vision, *Swarajya* must mean the Hindusthani *Swarajya.* All Hindus, Moslems, and other citizens have equal responsibilities, duties, and rights in such a *Swarajya*. However, such a *Swarajya* would not tolerate a particular community on religious grounds to get itself cut off from the Central Government and demand portions of the country. Moreover, in his view, any such aggressive claim on the part of a community would be immediately put down as 'an act of treachery' by the united strength of the Central Government.

Therefore, he opposed the demand of Muslims for the grant of a separate electorate in India. Having received such preferential treatment, he said that Muslims would probably be granted the right to exercise a veto on the legitimate rights and privileges of the majority. "The Hindus do not want a change of masters, are not going to ...fight and die only to replace an Edward by an Aurangzeb simply because the latter happens to be born within the Indian borders, but they want henceforth to be masters themselves in their own house, in their own land" (*ibid.*, 45).

As far as the Rights of non-Hindu Minorities is concerned, he maintains the principles of 'one man one vote'. In addition, public services will be awarded solely based on merit. Moreover, fundamental rights and obligations should be shared by all citizens alike irrespective of any distinction of race or religion. However, according to him, "...any further mention of minority rights is on principle not only unnecessary but self-contradictory, because it again introduces a consciousness of majority and minority on communal basis" (*ibid.*, 53). Thus, on the question of minority rights, the approach of Savarkar was in consonance with his broad conceptualization of the philosophy of Hindutva. Therefore, it is not surprising to see that he stated the crux of the Hindu Sanghatanist ideology in such a way, 'Hinduise all politics and Militarize Hindudom!'

Like Gandhi, Savarkar also provided a Constructive Programme (*ibid.*, 62). Particularly, he was concerned about the removal of untouchability like Gandhi and Ambedkar. His programme included intense efforts to conduct a whirlwind campaign in every village, town and city to remove untouchability. In his second programme, he proposes that all universities, colleges, and schools make military training compulsory to secure students' entry into the Naval, Aerial, and Military forces and institutions. His third programme included preparing the Hindu Electorate to the utmost measure possible to vote only for those Hindu 'Sanghatanists' who openly pledge to safeguard Hindu interests. From these, one might conclude that Savarkar was not only an armchair philosopher but a political activist also.

We may recall here, his programme of removal of untouchables was hailed by Gandhi also. Savarkar held the view that eradication of untouchability is the foremost and absolute *dharma*. He favoured to build pan-Hindu temples freely open to all Hindus irrespective of their caste rather than build separate and exclusive temples for untouchables. He was also in favour of opening old temples to all Hindus. The seemingly impossible task of eliminating untouchability is attainable with a change of mind that will unite Hindus. Thus, he mentioned "...that the removal of untouchability is a task as easy to be tackled as it is bound to strengthen Hindu consolidation. It will be nothing short of a victory won in the battlefield if we, within five years' time, can sweep out untouchability from the face of our country by killing the very idea of not touching our co-religionists on ground of birth in a particular caste alone, and removing automatically the special disability, some economical and some social, from which those of our religious brothers are suffering most unjustly at this hour. It is only a change of mentality and nothing more than that can achieve this seemingly insuperable task" (*ibid.*, 126).

NOTES

1. In the present study, the fifth edition has been used. The first edition of the book titled *Hindutva* published in May 1923 does not mention the name of Savarkar as its author. Instead of author of the text, it mentions 'A Martaha'. The reason is given in the second edition of the book as 'Veer Savarkar was still in prison and the author's name was not published'. The first edition also informs us that it was published by Sri V.V. Kelkar who was from Nagpur and it was printed in Poona city. In his notes, the publisher writes that the book's 'strong style', 'convincing arguments', 'passionate pleading', and 'able survey' will appeal even to those who disagree with the author. The publisher does not introduce the subject of

the book to the readers as the author is going to do it so beautifully in the coming pages. The first edition does not inform us anything about the author and context in which the book was written. It is also interesting to note that the first edition of the book was also translated into Hindi after three years. It was published in 1926 by Sri Lakshmannarayan Garde from Calcutta. The Preface by the Publisher of the second Edition of the book tells us about its discursive history. It notes that it was during his stay from 1906 to 1910 in England that the attention of Veer Savarkar was drawn pointedly to the question as to who can be precisely called a 'Hindu'. After years of study, he found the confusion lay in only identifying "Hindu" with religious aspects. Savarkar decided to approach this question historically. Savarkar wrote this book in prison, after he had come in contact with Khilafatists whose attitude apparently convinced him—a revolutionary till then—that Muslims were the real enemies, not the British.

2. The text begins with the problem and anxiety of naming. Thus, one may notice in the text that there is a rather strained, complex, confused and confusing argument for preferring Hindu rather than Bharat, and later a contemporary, transcendental political Hindutva rather than the hitherto diverse/sectarian polymorphous Hinduism.

REFERENCES

Savarkar, V.D. (1969). *Hindutva*. Bombay: Veer Savarkar Prakashan.

Savarkar, V.D. (2020). *Hindu Rashtra Darshan*, downloaded from https://fdocuments.in/download/hindu-rashtra-darshan-v-d-savarkarpdf.html

7
Three Worldviews of Hinduism

In this concluding chapter, we will juxtapose and evaluate Gandhi, Ambedkar, and Savarkar's vision of Hinduism. As all three were born Hindu, we will briefly compare their childhood exposure to Hinduism, assuming that it must have considerably shaped their notions of Hinduism. We will also briefly compare their intellectual development in a foreign land, as all these three geniuses spent their time outside India for higher studies. In our previous chapter, we have already discussed how these two factors significantly affected their views of Hinduism. Furthermore, these two factors help us to acknowledge their notions of Hinduism and to explore their interpretations of it in a proper light.

We noted Gandhi was born in an upper-class Hindu Vaishnava family and got his first introduction to Hinduism from his father and mother. His father and mother were 'deeply religious'. Although he was born in the Vaishnava faith, and he often had to visit the Haveli, it never appealed to him. But his introduction to the mythical story of Shravan made 'an indelible impression' on him. The Hindu mythological play Harish Chandra inspired him to 'follow truth' and 'go through all ordeals'. In his childhood, he learned to know about religion in part rather than through formal education in religion. It was his family nurse Rambha who sowed the seed of *Ramanama* that became an infallible remedy for him. Besides, reading *Ramayana* before his sick father also left a 'deep impression' on him. He attended the reading of another Hindu text the *Bhagavat*, but he found the reciter 'uninspiring'. He also got an early grounding in toleration for all branches of Hinduism and sister religions. This is because his father had many friends of different faiths and they used to come and discuss with him. He did not like *Manusmirti* which he read during his childhood. However, one thing that took deep root in his childhood was the conviction that 'morality is the basis of things, and that truth is the substance of all morality'. It is this childhood background in which

Gandhi could view Hinduism more liberally than the other two counterparts. Also, it was Rama, a symbol of the highest morality and duty in the Hindu religion, that became his ideal for his future.

Ambedkar was born in the Mahar family, an untouchable caste, of the Hindu religion. His family belonged to the devotional Kabir School of Thought which found consolation in human attributes like compassion, benevolence, and resignation to God. These devotees sought moral and spiritual satisfaction in Lord Krishna or Shri Rama. The Kabir School of Thought did not believe in the caste system and its founder Kabir condemned any kind of discrimination among human beings. Ambedkar's father lived a very 'industrious and intensely religious life'. His mother Bhimabai was a 'pious, gentle and self-respecting woman'. His mother came from a rich family and also belonged to the Kabir cult. Like Gandhi's father, Bhim's father also took a keen interest in 'religious and theological discussions'. He offered prayers and devotion to God, morning and evening. In his childhood, however, Ambedkar had to face the grim reality of untouchability prevalent in Hinduism. He had many bitter experiences of untouchability in his childhood and particularly in school days. His most important experience involved a journey from Satara to Koregaon in 1901, which gave him a shock that he had never experienced before, and made him think about untouchability. It was on this journey that he first encountered Hinduism's humiliation of untouchables. These childhood humiliations of Hinduism seem to become the bedrock of his later analysis of Hinduism. Further, it was Kabir, irrespective of religion and symbol of humanism, who became his ideal.

Savarkar, Maharashtrian like Ambedkar, and upper caste like Gandhi, was a Chitpavan Brahmin. It is a community that has produced Nana Shahib of 1857 fame, Vasudeo Balwant and Tilak. Like Gandhi's and Ambedkar's father, his father Damodar was a religious-minded man who kept a strict household. Growing up in a religious family, with a very pious and devout mother and father, Vinayak was exposed early to such texts as the *Mahabharata* and the *Ramayana*. These texts were often read aloud in the evenings by Damodar or one of his sons. From his early childhood, Savarkar was familiar with many epic heroes of Hindu culture, especially Shivaji, the Hindu warrior from Maharashtra. Vinayak was assigned by his father to offer customary daily worship to the household gods. There was an imposing and beautifully wrought brass image of Durga, around which centred a number of family traditions and myths. At her feet, he would sit for hours, at times so completely lost in communication as to loose all outward consciousness. It was Durga, goddess of power, who became the source of inspiration for him and Shivaji his ideal for his future life. Since childhood, he had been very curious about the political events in the country and used to ponder over their response. This eventually helped him to interpret Hinduism from a power and political standpoint.

All these three thinkers-leaders-activists spent considerable time in a foreign land for their higher studies. Gandhi spent three years in London (1888-91), Ambedkar three years in America (1913-16) and one year in London (1916-17), and Savarkar three years in London (1906-09). As we noted in the previous chapters, they were highly influenced by western thoughts and philosophy. The education they received in the West made them intellectually able to understand Hinduism.

We noted that Gandhi's views on Hinduism developed considerably in England (1888-91) and South Africa (1893-15). It is in London that he came across Theosophists and read Madame Blavatsky's *Key to Theosophy,* Edwin Arnold's *The Song Celestial* and *The Light of Asia,* and Carlyle's *Heroes and Hero-Worship.* Ironically, in shaping the idea of Hinduism, a Jain Raichanbhai also played a significant role in Gandhi's life. Raichanbhai's 'state of equipoise' left a deep impression on Gandhi, although he did not enthrone him as his *Guru.* Gandhi studied some Hindu texts in their original form in South Africa. He studied Swami Vivekananda's *Raja-yoga* and M.N. Dvivedi's *Rajayoga,* Patanjali's *Yoga Sutras.* In South Africa, Gandhi read Max Muller's book *India—What Can It Teach Us?* and the translation of the Upanishads published by the Theosophical Society. He also read Washington Irving's *Life of Mahomet and His Successors* and Carlyle's panegyric on the Prophet. Mahammad was raised in his estimation by these books. He also studied *The Sayings of Zarathustra.* In March 1905, he delivered the first of a series of four lectures on 'Hinduism' at the Masonic Temple. This was under the auspices of the Johannesburg Lodge of the Theosophical Society. Gandhi concluded the summary of his lecture series by pointing out 'an appeal to the audience'. He also provided the basis of all religions noting that 'all religions teach that we should all live together in love and mutual kindness'. As we may note, he saw Hinduism in the light of other religions and developed an inclusive understanding of religion. He realized that it is ethics that is the core of all religions and also common to every religion. Thus he developed a moral parameter to judge any religion and he judged Hinduism from the same point of view.

The time that Ambedkar spent in the USA was characterized by social liberation absent in India because of his untouchable status. As noted earlier, he read many philosophers in USA and London and was highly influenced by Jon Dewey, Bantham, Mill, and Garrison. We find many references to these thinkers in his writings. The philosophy of utilitarianism, pragmatism, and instrumentalism greatly inspired him and he used them to analyze social-economic reality. We may see that as the 'other West' influenced Gandhi while he was studying law in London, American thoughts of Dewey, James Shotwell, Edwin Seligman, James Harvey Robinson, Franklin Giddings, and Alexander Goldenweiser influenced Ambedkar in the same way. By them, Ambedkar received a broad and deep exposure to an optimistic, expansive, pragmatic body of knowledge. We noted he tried to analyze Hinduism also from the utility and justice point of view and exposed the problem of the caste system and untouchability ruthlessly. It is the pragmatic and instrumental approach that he learned in the USA that gave him the power to see the problem of Hinduism. This approach made him claim that 'inequality is the soul of Hinduism'.

Like Gandhi and Ambedkar, Savarkar also got exposure to Western knowledge traditions while studying law in London. Like Ambedkar, he was deeply influenced by European philosophers. He studied the philosophy and ideas of Political Economy of James Mill (1773-1836) and J. Stuart Mill (1806-76) in detail. Particularly, their concepts of liberalism, individual freedom, and ideas about democracy had a profound effect on his thinking. But the most relevant point is that he was highly impressed with the philosophy of evolution proposed by Herbert Spencer (1820-1903). From Herbert Spencer and Charles Darwin (1809-1882), he adopted the idea of the 'survival of the fittest' that underlies his social-political philosophy of Hindutva. His philosophical outlook was also strengthened by studying the works of Jeremy Bentham (1748-1832). He noted that after reading Bentham he began to acknowledge this principle of morality as the touchstone of all his pursuits, of his ethical standards, and his behaviour. He also got a sound understanding of the philosophy of Augusta Comte (1798-1857). From all these European authors, he learned the basic principles of social and political life. He interpreted them through Indian eyes, and used them to propose his best approach to the social and political problems of India. It all finally culminated in his political construction of Hindutva.

Different childhood exposure and different intellectual formations of these geniuses made them see Hinduism from three different angles. On this basis, they offer three different definitions of who is a Hindu? For Gandhi, "...In a concrete manner he is a Hindu who believes in God, immortality of the soul, transmigration, the law of *Karma* and *Moksha*, and who tries to practice Truth and Ahimsa in daily life, and therefore practices cow-protection in its widest sense and understands and tries to act according to the law of *Varnashrama*" (Gandhi, 1996: 3). On the other hand, Ambedkar mentioned, "...Ask a Parsi why he calls himself a Parsi, he will have no difficulty in answering the question. He will say he is a Parsi because he is a follower of Zoroaster. Ask the same question to a Christian. He too will have no difficulty in answering the question. He is a Christian because he believes in Jesus Christ. Put the same question to a Muslim. He too will have no hesitation in answering it. He will say he is a believer in Islam and that is why he is a Muslim. Now ask the same question to a Hindu and there is no doubt that he will be completely bewildered and would not know what to say... . The caste system is an essential feature of Hinduism and a man who does not belong to a recognised Hindu caste cannot be a Hindu" (BAWS 4: 13). And for Savarkar, "...[H]e is a Hindu to whom Sindhusthan is not only a *Pitribhu* but also a *Punyabhu*" (Savarkar, 1969: 110). In previous chapters, we saw how they reached these positions.

Finally, let us summarize the crux of the arguments advanced by these three thinkers-leaders-activists concerning Hinduism. We have already discussed them in detail in the earlier chapters. We also noted both context and text to see how they arrived at their respective positions. But here we juxtapose their central argument to get a clearer picture of their relative positions. This exercise of juxtaposing their ideas of Hinduism will help us see how their views on Hinduism are nonnegotiable, which was the principal argument advanced in this study.

Gandhi saw Hinduism through the moral lance and considered it as a relentless pursuit of truth through non-violent means. He noted that man may not believe even in God and still he may call himself a Hindu. He separated historical Hinduism from philosophical Hinduism. While historical Hinduism symbolizes untouchability, superstitious, worship of stocks and stones, animal sacrifice, and so on, philosophical Hinduism is the Hinduism of the *Gita*, the *Upanishads*, and Patanjali's *Yogasutras*. The philosophy of Hinduism is a culmination of *Ahimsa* and oneness. In his view, the chief value of Hinduism lies in holding the actual belief that all life, not only human beings but all sentient beings, is one. It means all life comes from one universal source, call it *Allah*, *God*, or *Parameshwara*. The unity of all life is a peculiarity of Hinduism. This is because it confines salvation not to human beings alone but says that it is possible for all God's creatures of all creation. For him, *Ahimsa* is the chief glory of Hinduism, and it has found the highest expression and application in Hinduism. He also saw it as the 'most tolerant of all religions' known to him. It provides the largest scope for self-expression to its votaries. For him Hinduism is not an exclusive religion. It enables the followers of that faith not merely to respect all religions, but also enables them to admire and assimilate whatever may be good in the other faiths.

Ambedkar viewed Hinduism from the perspective of utility and justice, and concluded that Hinduism is incompatible with the conditions for liberty to flourish. In his view, Hinduism is, therefore, a denial of liberty. It is also the denial of equality and the denial of the sacred character of human personality. In his framework, Hinduism is the gospel of superman and it teaches that what is right for superman is the only thing that is called morally right and morally good. On this ground, he claims that inequality is the soul of Hinduism. The morality of Hinduism is only social. He argued that the Hindu social order is an order based on graded classes in which the status and functions of the classes are determined and fixed and rigid. He noted three special features of the Hindu social order; the worship of the superman Brahmins, the denial of opportunity and right to education, and preventing rebellion against the social order, designed by God himself as sacred, so not open to abrogation, amendment, not even to criticism. In his view, the Caste System is not merely a division of labour but a division of labourers. It is a hierarchy in which the divisions of labourers are graded one above the other. Moreover, the Hindu Society is a myth. The name Hindu is itself foreign. It was given by the Mohammedans to the natives to distinguish themselves from them. In his framework, the problem lies not in the people, rather in the Hindu religion and its philosophy itself.

Influenced by the evolutionary philosophy of Herbert Spencer and the utilitarian ethics of J.S. Mill, Savarkar argued that an inquiry into what is Hinduism can only begin after the question 'who is a Hindu'. Moreover, it can only be answered by determining the essentials of Hindutva. He saw Hinduism as only a derivative, a fraction, a part of Hindutva. In his view, Hindutva embarrasses all the departments of thought and activity of the whole Being of the Hindu race. He gives historical proof of Indian or Hindu antiquity. Hindutva is not a word but a history, a history in full. In his view, Hindutva ran like a vital spinal cord through the whole body politic. The Hindus are not only a *Rashtra* and a *Jati*, but as a result, share a common *Sanskriti* as well. He claimed that everyone who is a Hindu inherits this *Sanskriti* and owes his spiritual being to it. He further noted that Hindus are bound together not only by the tie of the love they bear to a common fatherland and by the common blood that courses through their veins and keeps their hearts throbbing and their affections warm, but also by the tie of the common homage they pay to their great civilization—their Hindu culture. He noted these are the essentials of Hindutva—a common nation (*Rashtra*) a common race (*Jati*) and a common civilization (*Sanskriti*). All these essentials could best be summed up by stating in brief, as mentioned earlier, that he is a Hindu to whom Sindhusthan is not only a *Pitribhu* but also a *Punyabhu*". It is on this basis, Savarkar offered a political construct; Hindutva which is quite different from Gandhi and Ambedkar.

Gandhi offered a moral analysis of Hinduism based on nonviolence and truth, whereas Ambedkar offered a social analysis based on utility and justice. As for Savarkar, he offered a political analysis of Hinduism based on *rastra*, *jati*, and *sanskriti*. They also offered three prescriptions. Gandhi proposed a radical transformation of historical Hinduism and attempted to make it an inclusive ethical religion. Savarkar expected a Hindutva based on power, unity, and organization of Hindus. Ambedkar suggested leaving Hinduism for ever as it is nothing but inequality.

REFERENCES

Babasaheb Ambedkar: *Writings and Speeches* (*BAWS*), Vol. 4, New Delhi: Dr. Ambedkar Foundation, Ministry of Social Justice & Empowerment, Government of India.

Gandhi, M.K. (1996). *The Essence of Hinduism*. Ahmedabad: Navajivan.

Savarkar, V.D. (1969). *Hindutva*. Bombay: Veer Savarkar Prakashan.

Annexure -I

Gandhi's Article on *Hinduism*

[*Note*: Gandhi wrote the article Hinduism in *Young India*, 6-10-1921. He considered this article substantial and later on referred its many points in different speeches and letters. He clarified his claim of being a *sanatani* in this article which was opposed by many orthodox Hindus later on. It shows how Gandhi saw Hinduism]

In dealing with the problem of untouchability during the Madras tour, I have asserted my claim to being a Sanatani Hindu with greater emphasis than hitherto, and yet there are things which are commonly done in the name of Hinduism, which I disregard. I have no desire to be called a Sanatani Hindu or any other if I am not such. And I have certainly no desire to steal in a reform or an abuse under cover of a great faith.

It is, therefore, necessary for me once for all distinctly to give my meaning of *sanatana* Hinduism. The word *sanatana* I use in its natural sense. I call myself a sanatani Hindu, because,

1. I believe in the Vedas, the Upanishads, the Puranas and all that goes by the name of Hindu scriptures, and therefore in avatars and rebirth,
2. I believe in the varnashrama dharma in a sense in my opinion strictly Vedic but not in its present popular and crude sense,
3. I believe in the protection of the cow in its much larger sense than the popular, and
4. I do not disbelieve in idol-worship.

The reader will note that I have purposely refrained from using the word divine origin in reference to the Vedas or any other scriptures. For I do not believe in the exclusive divinity of the Vedas. I believe the Bible, the Koran, and the Zend-Avesta to be as much divinely inspired as the Vedas. My belief in the Hindu scriptures does not require me to accept every word and every verse as divinely inspired. Nor do I claim to have any first-hand knowledge of these wonderful books. But I do claim to know and feel the truths of the essential teaching of the scriptures. I decline to be bound by any interpretation, however learned it may be, if it is repugnant to reason or moral sense. I do most emphatically repudiate the claim (if they advance any such) of the present Shankaracharyas and Shastris to give a correct interpretation of the Hindu scriptures. On the contrary I believe, that our present knowledge of these books is in a most chaotic state. I believe implicitly in the Hindu aphorism, that no one truly knows the Shastras who has not attained perfection in innocence (*ahimsa*), truth (*satya*) and self-control (*brahmacharya*) and who has not renounced all acquisitions or possessions of wealth. I believe in the institution of gurus, but in this age millions must go without a guru, because it is a rare thing to find a combination of perfect purity and perfect learning. But one needs no despair of ever knowing the truth of one's religion, because the fundamentals of Hinduism as of every great religion are unchangeable, and easily understood. Every Hindu believes in God and his oneness, in rebirth and salvation. But that which distinguishes Hinduism from every other religion is its cow-protection, more than its *varnashrama*.

Varnashrama is, in my opinion, inherent in human nature, and Hinduism has simply reduced it to a science. It does attach to birth. A man cannot change his *varna* by choice. Not to abide by one's varna is to disregard the law of heredity. The division, however, into innumerable castes is an unwarranted liberty taken with the doctrine. The four divisions are all-sufficing.

I do not believe, that inter-dining or even inter-marriage necessarily deprives a man of his status that his birth has given him. The four divisions define a man's calling, they do not restrict or regulate social intercourse. The divisions define duties, they confer no privileges. It is, I hold, against the genius of Hinduism to arrogate to oneself a higher status or assign to another a lower. All are born to serve God's creation, a Brahmin with his knowledge, a Kshatriya with his power of protection, a Vaisya with his commercial ability and a Shudra with his bodily labour. This, however, does not mean that a Brahmin for instance is absolved from bodily labour, or the duty of protecting himself and others. His birth makes a Brahmin predominantly a man of knowledge, the fittest by heredity and training to impart it to others. There nothing, again, to prevent the Shudra from acquiring all the knowledge he wishes. Only, he will best serve with his body and need not envy others their special qualities for service. But a Brahmin who claims superiority by right of knowledge falls and has no knowledge. And so with the others who pride themselves their special qualities. Varnashrama is self-restraint and conservation and economy of energy.

Thought therefore, *varnashrama* is not affected by inter-dining or inter-marriage, Hinduism does most emphatically discourage inter-dining and inter-marriage between divisions. Hinduism reached the highest limit of self-restraint. It is undoubtedly a religion of renunciation of tile flesh so that the spirit may be set free. It is no part of a Hindu's duty to dine with his son. And by restricting his choice of a bride to a particular group, he exercises rare self-restraint. Hinduism does not regard a married state as by any means essential for salvation. Marriage is a "fall" even as birth is a "fall". Salvation is freedom from birth and hence death also. Prohibition against inter-marriage and inter-dining is essential for a rapid evolution of the soul. But this self-denial is no test of *varna*. A Brahmin may remain a Brahmin, though he may dine with his Shudra brother, if he has not left off his duty of service by knowledge. It follows from what I have said above, that restraint in matters of marriage and dining is not based upon notions of superiority. A Hindu who refuses to dine with another from a sense of superiority misrepresents his *dharma*.

Unfortunately, today Hinduism seems to consist merely in eating and not-eating. Once I horrified a pious Hindu by taking toast at a Mussulman's house. I saw, that he was pained to see me pouring milk into a cup handed by a Mussulman friend, but his anguish knew no bounds when he saw me taking toast at the Mussulman's hands. Hinduism is in danger of losing its substance if it resolves itself into a matter of elaborate rules as to what and with whom to eat. Abstemiousness from intoxicating drinks and drugs, and from all kinds of foods, especially meat, is undoubtedly a great aid to the evolution of the spirit, but it is by no means an end in itself. Many a man eating meat and with everybody but living in the fear of God is nearer his freedom than a man religiously abstaining from meat and many other things, but blaspheming God in everyone of his acts.

The central fact of Hinduism, however, is cow-protection. Cow-protection to me is one of the most wonderful phenomena in human evolution. It takes the human being beyond his species. The cow to me means the entire sub-human world. Man through the cow is enjoined to realize his identity with all that lives. Why the cow was selected for apotheosis is obvious to me. The cow was in India the best companion. She was the giver of plenty. Not only did she give milk, but she also made agriculture possible. The cow is a poem of pity. One reads pity in the gentle animal. She is the mother to millions of Indian mankind. Protection of the cow means protection of the whole dumb creation of God. The ancient seer, whoever he was, began with the cow. The appeal of the lower order of creation is all the more forcible because it is speechless. Cow-protection is the gift of Hinduism to the world. And Hinduism will live so long as there are Hindus to protect the cow.

The way to protect is to die for her. It is a denial of Hinduism in and *ahimsa* to kill a human being to protect a cow. Hindus are enjoined to protect the cow by their *tapasya*, by self-purification, by self-sacrifice. The present-day cow-protection has degenerated into a perpetual feud with the Mussulmans, whereas cow-protection means conquering Mussulmans by our love. A Mussulman friend sent me some time ago a book detailing the inhumanities practised by us on the cow and her progeny. How we bleed her to take the last drop of milk from her, how we starve her to emaciation, how we ill-treat the calves, how we deprive them of their portion of milk, how cruelly we treat the oxen, how we castrate them, how we beat them, how we overload them. If they had speech, they would bear witness to our crimes against them which would stagger the world. By every act of cruelty to our cattle, we disown God and Hinduism. I do not know that the condition of the cattle in any other part of the world is so bad as in unhappy India. We may not blame the Englishman for this. We may not plead poverty in our defence. Criminal negligence is the only cause of the miserable condition of our cattle. Our pinjrapoles, though they are an answer to our instinct of mercy, are a clumsy demonstration of its execution. Instead of being model dairy farms and great profitable national institutions, they are merely depots for receiving decrepit cattle.

Hindus will be judged not by their *tilaks*, not by the correct chanting of *mantras*, not by their pilgrimages, not by their most punctilious observance of caste rules but by their ability to protect the cow. Whilst professing the religion of cow-protection, we have enslaved the cow and her progeny, and have become slaves ourselves.

It will now be understood why I consider myself a sanatani Hindu. I yield to none in my regard for the cow. I have made the Khilafat cause my own, because I see that through its preservation full protection can be secured for the cow. I do not ask my Mussulman friends to save the cow in consideration of my service. My prayer ascends daily to God Almighty, that my service of a cause I hold to be just may appear so pleasing to Him, that He may change the hearts of the Mussulmans, and fill them with pity for their Hindu neighbours and make them save the animal the latter hold dear as life itself.

I can no more describe my feeling for Hinduism than for my own wife. She moves me as no other woman in the world can. Not that she has no fault. I dare say she has many more than I see myself. But the feeling of an indissoluble bond is there. Even so I feel for and about Hinduism with all its faults and limitations. Nothing elates me so much as the music of the *Gita* or the *Ramayana* by Tulsidas, the only two books in Hinduism I may be said to know. When I fancied I was taking my last breath, the *Gita* was my solace. I know the vice that is going on today in all the great Hindu shrines, but I love them in spite of their unspeakable failings. There is an interest which I take in them and which I take in no other. I am a reformer through and through. But my zeal never takes me to the rejection of any of the essential things of Hinduism. I have said I do not disbelieve in idol-worship. An idol does not excite any feeling of veneration in me. But I think that idol-worship is part of human nature. We hanker after symbolism. Why should one be more composed in a church than elsewhere? Images are an aid to worship. No Hindu considers an image to he God. I do not consider idol-worship a sin.

It is clear from the foregoing, that Hinduism is not an exclusive religion. In it there is room for the worship of all the prophets of the world. It is not a missionary religion in the ordinary sense of the term. It has no doubt absorbed many tribes in its fold, but this absorption has been of an evolutionary imperceptible character. Hinduism tells everyone to worship God according to his own faith or *dharma*, and so it lives at peace with all the religions.

That being my conception of Hinduism, I have never been able to reconcile myself to untouchability. I have always regarded it as an excrescence. It is true that it has been handed down to us from generations, but so are many evil practices even to this day. I should be ashamed to think that dedication of girls to virtual prostitution was a part of Hinduism. Yet it is practised by Hindus in many parts of India. I consider it positive irreligion to sacrifice goats to Kali and do not consider it a part of Hinduism. Hinduism is a growth of ages. The very name, Hinduism, was given to the religion of the people of Hindustan by foreigners. There was no doubt at one time sacrifice of animals offered in the name of religion. But It is not religion, much less is it Hindu religion. And so also it seems to me, that when cow-protection became an article of faith with our ancestors, those who persisted in eating beef were excommunicated. The civil strife must have been fierce. Social boycott was applied not only to the recalcitrants, but their sins were visited upon their children also. The practice which had probably its origin in good intentions hardened into usage, and even verses crept in our sacred books giving the practice a permanence wholly undeserved and still less justified. Whether my theory is correct or not, untouchability is repugnant to reason and to the instinct of mercy, pity or love. A religion that establishes the worship of the cow cannot possibly countenance or warrant a cruel and inhuman boycott of human beings. And I should be content to be torn to pieces rather than disown the suppressed classes. Hindus will certainly never deserve freedom, nor get it if they allow their noble religion to be disgraced by the retention of the taint of untouchability. And as I love Hinduism dearer than life itself, the taint has become for me an intolerable burden. Let us not deny God by denying to a fifth of our race the right of association on an equal footing.

[*Source*: CWMG 21: 245-50]

Annexure -II

Ambedkar's Historic Speech during Mahad Agitation

[*Note:* This is historic speech by Dr. Ambedkar given on 25 December, 1927. The context of the speech was an agitation by the Dalits to draw water from the Chavadar lake at Mahad. The water of this lake was hitherto reserved for caste Hindus. The following is the speech made by Dr. Ambedkar on this occasion. This speech shows Ambedkar's views on Hinduism in nutshell].

Gentlemen, you have gathered here today in response to the invitation of the Satyagraha Committee. As the Chairman of that Committee, I gratefully welcome you all.

Many of you will remember that on the 19th of last March all of us came to the Chavadar Lake here. The caste Hindus of Mahad had laid no prohibition on us; but they showed they had objections to our going there by the attack they made. The fight brought results that one might have expected. The aggressive caste Hindus were sentenced to four months' rigorous imprisonment, and are now in jail. If we had not been hindered on 19th March, it would have been proved that the caste Hindus acknowledge our right to draw water from the lake, and we should have had no need to begin our present undertaking.

Unfortunately we were thus hindered, and we have been obliged to call this meeting today. This lake at Mahad is public property. The caste Hindus of Mahad are so reasonable that they not only draw water from the lake themselves but freely permit people of any religion to draw water from it, and accordingly people of other religions such as the Islamic do make use of this permission. Nor do the caste Hindus prevent members of species considered lower than the human, such as birds and beasts, from drinking at the lake. Moreover, they freely permit beasts kept by untouchables to drink at the lake.

Caste Hindus are the very founts of compassion. They practice no *hinsa* and harass no one. They are not of the class of miserly and selfish folk who would grudge even a grow some grains of the food they are eating. The proliferation of *sanyasis* and mendicants is a living testimony to their charitable temperament. They regard altruism as religious merit and injury to another as a sin.

Even further, they have imbibed the principle that injury done by another must not be repaid but patiently endured, and so, they not only treat the harmless cow with kindness, but spare harmful creatures such as snakes. That one *Atman* or Spiritual Self dwells in all creatures has become a settled principle of their conduct. Such are the caste Hindus who forbid some human beings of their own religion to draw water from the same Chavadar Lake! One cannot help asking the question, why do they forbid us alone?

It is essential that all should understand thoroughly the answer to this question. Unless you do, I feel, you will not grasp completely the importance of today's meeting. The Hindus are divided, according to sacred tradition, into four castes; but according to custom, into five: Brahmins, Kshatriyas, Vaishyas, Shudras and Atishudras. The caste system is the first of the governing rules of the Hindu religion. The second is that the castes are of unequal rank. They are ordered in a descending series of each meaner than the one before.

Not only are their ranks permanently fixed by the rule, but each is assigned boundaries it must not transgress, so that each one may at once be recognized as belonging to its particular rank. There is a general belief that the prohibitions in the Hindu religion against intermarriage, interdining, interdrinking and social intercourse are bounds set to degrees of association with one another. But this is an incomplete idea. These prohibitions are indeed limits to degrees of association; but they have been set to show people of unequal rank what the rank of each is. That is, these bounds are symbols of inequality.

Just as the crown on a man's head shows he is a king, and the bow in his hand shows him to be a Kshatriya, the class to which none of the prohibitions applies is considered the highest of all and the one to which they all apply is reckoned the lowest in rank. The strenuous efforts made to maintain the prohibitions are for the reason that, if they are relaxed, the inequality settled by religion will break down and equality will take its place. The caste Hindus of Mahad prevent the untouchables from drinking the water of the Chavadar Lake not because they suppose that the touch of the untouchables will pollute the water or that it will evaporate and vanish. Their reason for preventing the untouchables from drinking it is that they do not wish to acknowledge by such a permission that castes declared inferior by sacred tradition are in fact their equals.

Gentlemen! you will understand from this the significance of the struggle we have begun. Do not let yourselves suppose that the Satyagraha Committee has invited you to Mahad merely to drink the water of the Chavadar Lake of Mahad.

It is not as if drinking the water of the Chavadar Lake will make us immortal, We have survived well enough all these days without drinking it. We are not going to the Chavadar Lake merely to drink its water. We are going to the Lake to assert that we too are human beings like others. It must be clear that this meeting has been called to set up the norm of equality. I am certain that no one who thinks of this meeting in this light will doubt that it is unprecedented. I feel that no parallel to it can be found in the history of India. If we seek for another meeting in the past to equal this, we shall have to go to the history of France on the continent of Europe. A hundred and thirty-eight years ago, on 24 January, 1789, King Louis XVI had convened, by royal command, an assembly of deputies to represent the people of the kingdom. "his French National Assembly has been much vilified by historians. The Assembly sent the King and the Queen of France to the guillotine; persecuted and massacred the aristocrats; and drove their survivors into exile. It confiscated the estates of the rich and plunged Europe into war for fifteen years. Such are the accusations levelled against the Assembly by the historians. In my view, the criticism is misplaced; further, the historians of this school have not understood the gist of the achievement of the French National Assembly. That achievement served the welfare not only of France but of the entire European continent. If European nations enjoy peace and prosperity today, it is for one reason: the revolutionary French National Assembly convened in 1789 set new principles for the organization of society before the disorganized and decadent French nation of its time, and the same principles have been accepted and followed by Europe.

To appreciate the importance of the French National Assembly and the greatness of its principles, we must keep in mind the suite of French society at the time. You are all aware that our Hindu society is based on the system of castes. A rather similar system of classes existed in the France of 1789: the difference was that it was a society of there castes. Like the Hindu society, the French had a class of Brahmins and another of Kshatriyas. But instead of three different castes of Vaishya, Shudra and Atishudra, there was one class that comprehended these. This is a minor difference. The important thing is that the caste or class system was similar. The similarity to be noted is not only in the differentiation between classes: the inequality of our caste system was also to be found in the French social system. The nature of the inequality in the French society was different: it was economic in nature. It was, however, equally intense. The thing to bear in mind is there is a great similarity between the French National Assembly that met on 5 May, 1789 at Versailles and our meeting today. The similarity is not only in the circumstances in which the two meetings took place but also in their ideals.

That Assembly of the French people was convened to reorganize French society. Our meeting today too has been convened to reorganize Hindu society. Hence, before discussing on what principles our society should be reorganized, we should all pay heed to the principles on which the French Assembly relied and the policy it adopted. The scope of the French Assembly was far wider than that of our present meeting. It had to carry out the threefold organization of the French political, social and religious systems. We must confine ourselves to how social and religious reorganization can be brought about. Since we are not, for the present, concerned with political reorganization, let us see what the French Assembly did in the matter of the religious and social reorganization of their nation. The policy adopted by the French National Assembly in this area can be seen plainly by anyone from three important proclamations issued by that Assembly. The first was issued on 17 June, 1789. This was a proclamation about the class systems in France. As said before, French society was divided into three classes. The proclamation abolished the three classes and blended them into one. Further, it abolished the seats reserved separately for the three classes (or estates) in the political assembly. The second proclamation was about the priests. By ancient custom, to appoint or remove these priests was outside the power of the nation, that being the monopoly of a foreign religious potentate, the Pope. Anyone appointed by the Pope was a priest, whether or not he was fit to be one in the eyes of those to whom he was to preach. The proclamation abolished the autonomy of the religious orders and assigned to the French nation the authority to decide who might follow this vocation, who was fit for it and who was not, whether he was to be paid for preaching or not, and so on. The third proclamation was not about the political, economic or religious systems. It was of a general nature and laid down the principles on which all social arrangements ought to rest. From that point of view, the third proclamation is the most important of the three; it might be called the king of these proclamations. It is renowned the worldover as the declaration of human birthrights. It is not only unprecedented in the history of France; more than that, it is unique in the history of civilized nations. For every European nation has followed the French Assembly in giving it a place in its own Constitution. So one may say that it brought about a revolution not only in France but the whole world. This proclamation has seventeen clauses, of which the following are important:

1. All human beings are equal by birth; and they shall remain equal till death. They may be distinguished in status only in the public interest. Otherwise, their equal status must be maintained.
2. The ultimate object of politics is to maintain these human birthrights.
3. The entire nation is the mother-source of sovereignty. The rights of any individual, group or special class, unless they are given by the nation, cannot be acknowledged as valid on any other ground, be it political or religious.
4. Any person is free to act according to his birthright. Any limit placed upon this freedom must be only to the extent necessary to permit other persons to enjoy their birthrights. Such limits must be laid down by law: they cannot be set on the grounds of the religion or on any other basis than the law of the land.
5. The law will forbid only such actions as are injurious to society. All must be free to do what has not been forbidden by law. Nor can anyone be compelled to do what the law has not laid down as a duty.
6. The law is not in the nature of bounds set by any particular class. The right to decide what the law shall be rest with the people or their representatives. Whether such a law is protective or punitive, it must be the same for all. Since justice requires that all social arrangements be based on the equality of all, all individuals are equally eligible for any kind of honour, power and profession. Any distinction in such matters must be owing to differences of individual merit; it must not be based on birth.

I feel our meeting today should keep the image of this French National Assembly before the mind. The road it marked out for the development of the French nation, the road that all progressed nations have followed, ought to be the road adopted for the development of Hindu society by this meeting. We need to pull away the nails which hold the framework of caste-bound Hindu society together, such as those of the prohibition of intermarriage down to the prohibition of social intercourse so that Hindu society becomes all of one caste. Otherwise untouchability cannot be removed nor can equality be established.

Some of you may feel that since we are untouchables, it is enough if we are set free from the prohibitions of inter drinking and social intercourse. That we need not concern ourselves with the caste system; how does it matter if it remains? In my opinion this is a total error. If we leave the caste system alone and adopt only the removal of untouchability as our policy, people will say that we have chosen a low aim. To raise men, aspiration is needed as much as outward efforts. Indeed it is to be doubted whether efforts are possible without aspiration. Hence, if a great effort is to be made, a great aspiration must be nursed. In adopting an aspiration one need not be abashed or deterred by doubts about one's power to satisfy it. One should be ashamed only of mean aspirations; not of failure that may result because one's aspiration is high. If untouchability alone is removed, we may change from Atishudras to Shurdas; but can we say that this radically removes untouchability? If such puny reforms as the removal of restrictions on social intercourse etc., were enough for the eradication of untouchability, I would not have suggested that the caste system itself must go. Gentlemen! you all know that if a snake is to be killed it is not enough to strike at its tail—its head must be crushed. If any harm is to be removed, one must seek out its root and strike at it. An attack must be based on the knowledge of the enemy's vital weakness. Duryodhana was killed because Bheema struck at his thigh with his mace. If the mace had hit Duryodhana's head he would not have died; for his thigh was his vulnerable spot. One finds many instances of a physician's efforts to remove a malady proving fruitless because he has not perceived fully what will get rid of the disease; similar instances of failure to root out a social disease muse it is not fully diagnosed are rarely recorded in history; and so one does not often become aware of them. But let me acquaint you with one such instance that I have come across in my reading. In the ancient European nation of Rome, the patricians were considered upper class, and the plebians, lower class. All power was in the hands of, the patricians, and they used it to ill-treat the plebians. To free themselves from this harassment, the plebians, on the strength of their unity, insisted that laws should be written down for the facilitation of justice and for the information of all. Their patrician opponents agreed to this; and a charter of twelve laws was written down. But this did not rid the oppressed plebians of their woes. For the officers who enforced the laws were all of the patrician class; moreover the chief officer, called the tribune, was also a patrician. Hence, though the laws were uniform, there was partiality in their enforcement. The plebians then demanded that instead of the administration being in the hands of one tribune there should be two tribunes, of whom one should be elected by the plebians and the other by the patricians. The patricians yielded to this too, and the plebians rejoiced, supposing they would now be free of their miseries. But their rejoicing was short-lived. The Roman people had a tradition that nothing was to be done without the favourable verdict of the oracle at Delphi. Accordingly, even the election of a duly elected tribune—if the oracle did not approve of him—had to be treated as annulled, and another had to be elected, of whom the oracle approved. The priest who put the question to the oracle was required, by sacred religious custom, to be one born of parents married in the mode the Romans called *conferatio;* and this mode of marriage prevailed only among the patricians; so that the priest of Delphi was always a patrician.

The wily priest always saw to it that if the plebians elected a man really devoted to their cause, the oracle went against him. Only if the man elected by the plebians to the position of tribune was amenable to the patricians, would the oracle favour him and give him the opportunity of actually assuming office. What did the plebians gain by their right to elect a tribune? The answer must be, nothing in reality. Their efforts proved meaningless because they did not trace the malady to its source. If they had, they would, at the same time that they demanded a tribune of their election, have also settled the question of who should be the priest at Delphi. The disease could not be eradicated by demanding a tribune; it needed control of the priestly office; which the plebians failed to perceive. We too, while we seek a way to remove untouchability, must inquire closely into what will eradicate the disease; otherwise we too may miss our aim. Do not be foolish enough to believe that removal of the restrictions on social intercourse or interdrinking will remove untouchability.

Remember that if the prohibitions on social intercourse and interdrinking go, the roots of untouchability are not removed. Release from these two restrictions will, at the most, remove untouchability as it appears outside the home; but it will leave untouchability in the home untouched. If we want to remove untouchability in the home as well as outside, we must break down the prohibition against intermarriage. Nothing else will serve. From another point of view, we see that breaking down the bar against intermarriage is the way to establish real equality. Anyone must confess that when the root division is dissolved, incidental points of separateness will disappear by themselves. The interdictions on interdining, interdrinking and social intercourse have all sprung from the one interdiction against intermarriage. Remove the last and no special efforts are needed to move the rest. They will disappear of their own accord. In my view the removal of untouchability consists in breaking down the ban on intermarriage and doing so will establish real equality. If we wish to mt out untouchability, we must recognize that the root of untouchability is in the ban on intermarriage. Even if our attack today is on the ban against interdrinking, we must press it home against the ban on intermarriage; otherwise untouchability cannot be removed by the toots. Who can accomplish this task? It is no Secret that the Brahmin class cannot do it. While the caste system lasts, the Brahmin caste has its supremacy. No one, of his own will, surrenders power which is in his hands. The Brahmins have exercised their sovereignty over all other castes for centuries. It is not likely that they will be willing to give it up and treat the rest as equals. The Brahmins do not have the patriotism of the Samurais of Japan. It is useless to hope that they will sacrifice their privileges as the Samurai class did, for the sake of national unity based on a new equality. Nor does it appear likely that the task will be carried out by other caste Hindus. These others, such as the class comprising the Marathas and other similar castes, are a class between the privileged and those without any rights.

A privileged class, at the cost of a little self-sacrifice, can show some generosity. A class without any privileges has ideals and aspirations; for, at least as a matter of self-interest, it wishes to bring about a social reform. As a result it develops an attachment to principles rather than to self-interest. The class of caste Hindus other than Brahmins Lies in between: it cannot practise the generosity possible to the class above and it does not develop the attachment to prnciples that develops in the class below. This is why this class is seen to be concerned not so much about attaining equality with the Brahmins as about maintaining its status above the untouchables.

For the purposes of the social reform required, the class of caste Hindus other than Brahmins is feeble. If we are to await its help, we should fall into the difficulties that the farmer faced, who depended on his neighbour's help for his harvesting, as in the story of the mother lark and her chicks found in many textbooks.

The task of removing untouchability and establishing equality that we have undertaken, we must carry out ourselves. Others will not do it. Our life will gain its true meaning if we consider that we are born to carry out this task and set to work in earnest. Let us receive this merit which is awaiting us.

This is a struggle in order to raise ourselves; hence we are bound to undertake it, so as to remove the obstacles to our progress. We all know how at every turn, untouchability muddies and soils our whole existence. We know that at one time our people were recruited in large numbers into the troops. It was a kind of occupation socially assigned to us and few of us needed to be anxious about earning our bread. Other classes of our level have found their way into the troops, the police, the courts and the offices, to earn their bread. But in the same areas of employment you will no longer find the untouchables.

It is not that the law debars us from these jobs. Everything is permissible as far the law is concerned. But the Government finds itself powerless because other Hindus consider us untouchables and look down upon us, and it acquiesces in our being kept out of Government jobs. Nor can we take up any decent trade. It is true, partly, that we lack money to start business, but the real difficulty is that people regard us as untouchables and no one will accept goods from our hands.

To sum up, untouchability is not a simple matter; it is the mother of all our poverty and lowliness and it has brought us to the abject state we are in today. If we want to raise ourselves out of it, we must undertake this task. We cannot be saved in any other way. It is a task not for our benefit alone; it is also for the benefit of the nation.

Hindu society must sink unless the untouchability that has become a part of the four-caste system is eradicated. Among the resources that any society needs in the struggle for life, a great resource is the moral order of that society. And everyone must admit that a society in which the existing moral order upholds things that disrupt the society and condemns those that would unite the members of the society, must find itself defeated in any struggle for life with other societies. A society which has the opposite moral order, one in which things that unite are considered laudable and things that divide are condemned, is sure to succeed in any such struggle.

This principle must be applied to Hindu society. Is it any wonder that it meets defeat at every turn when it upholds a social order that fragments its members, though it is plain to anyone who sees it that the four-caste system is such a divisive force and that a single caste for all, would unite society? If we wish to escape these disastrous conditions, we must break down the framework of the four-caste system and replace it by a single caste system.

Even this will not be enough. The inequality inherent in the four-caste system must be rooted out. Many people mock at the principles of equality. Naturally, no man is another's equal. One has an impressive physique; another is slow-witted. The mockers think that, in view of these inequalities that men are born with, the egalitarians are absurd in telling us to regard them as equals. One is forced to say that these mockers have not understood fully the principle of equality.

If the principle of equality means that privilege should depend, nor on birth, wealth, or anything else, but solely on the merits of each man, then how can it be demanded that a man without merit, and who is duty and vicious, should be treated on a level with a man who has merit and is clean and virtuous? Such is a counter-question sometimes posed. It is essential to define equality as giving equal privileges to men of equal merit. But before people have had an opportunity to develop their inherent qualities and to merit privileges, it is just to treat them all equally. In sociology, the social order is itself the most important factor in the full development of qualities that any person may possess at birth. If slaves are constantly treated unequally, they will develop no qualities other than those appropriate to slaves, and they wilt never become fit for any higher status. If the clean man always repulses the unclean man and refuses to have anything to do with him, the unclean man will never develop the aspiration to become clean. If the criminal or immoral castes are given no refuge by the virtuous castes, the criminal castes will never learn virtue.

The examples given above show that, although an equal treatment may not create good qualities in one who does not have them at all, even such qualities where they exist need equal treatment for their development; also, developed good qualities are wasted and frustrated without equal treatment.

On the one hand, the inequality in Hindu society stuns the progress of individuals and in consequence stunts society. On the other hand, the same inequality prevents society from bringing into use powers stored in individuals. In both ways, this inequality is weakening Hindu society, which is in disarray because of the four-castes system.

Hence, if Hindu society is to be strengthened, we must uproot the four-caste system and untouchability, and set the society on the foundations of the two principles of one caste only and of equality. The way to abolish untouchability is not any other than the way to invigorate Hindu society. Therefore, I say that our work is beyond doubt as much for the benefit of the nation as it is in our own interest. Our work has been begun to bring about a real social revolution. Let no one deceive himself by supposing that it is a diversion to quieten minds entranced with sweet words. The work is sustained by strong feeling, which is the power that drives the movement. No one can now arrest it. I pray to God that the social revolution which begins here today may fulfil itself by peaceful means.

None can doubt that the responsibility of letting the revolution take place peacefully rats more heavily on our opponents than on us. Whether this social revolution will work peacefully or violently will depend wholly on the conduct of the caste Hindus. People who blame the French National Assembly of 1789 for atrocities forget one thing. That is, if the rulers of France had not been treacherous to the Assembly, if the upper classes had not resisted it, had not committed the crime of trying to suppress it with foreign help, it would have had no need to use violence in the work of the revolution and the whole social transformation would have been accomplished peacefully.

We say to our opponents too: please do not oppose us. Put away the orthodox scriptures. Follow justice. And we assure you that we shall carry out our programme peacefully.

[*Sources*: http://www.cscsarchive.org/dataarchive/otherfiles/ TA001003/file]

Annexure-III

Savarkar on Hinduism and Hindutva and Who is Hindu ?

[*Note:* Here two central sub sections chapters of Savarkar's text Hindutva have been given to grasp Savarkar's political construct of Hindutva].

Hinduism and Hindutva

Hindutva is different from Hinduism. To this category of names which have been to mankind a subtle source of life and inspiration belongs to the word Hindutva, the essential nature and significance of which we have to investigate into. The ideas and ideals, the systems and societies, the thoughts and sentiments which have centred round this name are so varied and rich, so powerful and so subtle, so elusive and yet so vivid that the term Hindutva defies all attempts at analysis. Forty centuries, if not more, had been at work to mould it as it is. Prophets and poets, lawyers and law-givers, heroes and historians, have thought, lived, fought and died just to have it spelled thus. For indeed, is it not the resultant of countless actions—now conflicting, now commingling, now cooperating—of our whole race? Hindutva is not a word but a history. Not only the spiritual or religious history of our people as at times it is mistaken to be by being confounded with the other cognate term Hinduism, but a history in full. Hinduism is only a derivative, a fraction, a part of Hindutva. Unless it is made clear what is meant by the latter the first remains unintelligible and vague. Failure to distinguish between these two terms has given rise to much misunderstanding and mutual suspicion between some of those sister communities that have inherited this inestimable and common treasure of our Hindu civilization. What is the fundamental difference in the meaning of these two words would be clear as our arguement proceeds. Here it is enough to point out that Hindutva is not identical with what is vaguely indicated by the term Hinduism. By an 'ism' it is generally meant a theory or a code more or less based on spiritual or religious dogma or creed. Had not linguistic usage stood in our way then 'Hinduness' would have certainly been a better word than Hinduism as a near parallel to Hindutva. Hindutva embrases all the departments of thought and activity of the whole Being of our Hindu race. Therefore, to understand the significance of this term Hindutva, we must first understand the essential meaning of the word Hindu itself and realize how it came to exercise such imperial sway over the hearts of millions of mankind and won a loving allegiance from the bravest and best of them. But before we can do that, it is imperative to point out that we are by no means attempts on a definition or even a description of the more limited, less satisfactory and essentially sectarian term Hinduism. How far we can succeed or are justified in doing that would appear as we proceed.

Who is a Hindu?

Who is a Hindu ? The words Hindutva and Hinduism both of them being derived from the word Hindu, must necessarily be understood to refer to the whole of the Hindu people. Any definition of Hinduism that leaves out any important section of our people and forces them either to play false to their convictions or to go outside the pale of Hindutva stands self-condemned. Hinduism means the system of religious beliefs found common amongst the Hindu people. And the only way to find out what those religious beliefs of the Hindus are, i.e. what constitutes Hinduism, you must first define a Hindu. But forgetting this chief implication of the word, Hinduism which clearly presupposes an independent conception of a Hindu many people go about to determine the essentials of Hinduism and finding none so satisfactory as to include, without overlapping all our Hindu communities, come to the desperate conclusion—which does not satisfy them either—that, therefore, those communities are not Hindus at all; not because the definition they had framed is open to the fault of exclusion but because those communities do not subject themselves to the required tenets which these gentlemen have thought it fit to label as 'Hinduism'. This way of answering the question 'who is a Hindu' is really prepostereus and has given rise to so much of bitterness amongst some of our brethren of Avaidik school of thought, the Sikh, the Jain, the Devsamaji and even our patriotic and progressive Aryasamajis.

'Who is a Hindu ?' —he who is subject to the tenets of Hinduism. Very well. What is Hinduism ? —those tenets to which the Hindus are subjected. This is very nearly arguing in a circle and can never lead to a satisfactory solution. Many of our friends who have been on this wrong track have come back to tell us 'there are no such people as Hindus at all!' If some Indians, as gifted as that Englishman who first coined the word Hinduism, coins a parallel word 'Englishism' and proceeds to find out the underlying unity of beliefs amongst the English people, gets disgusted with thousands of sects and societies from Jews to the Jacobins, from Trinity to Utility, and comes out to announce that 'there are no such people as the English at all,' he would not make himself more ridiculous than those who declare in cold print' there is nothing as a Hindu people.' Anyone who wants to see what a confusion of thought prevails on the point and how the failure to analyse separately the two terms Hindutva and Hinduism renders that confusion worst confounded may do well to go through the booklet 'Essentials of Hinduism' published by the enterprising 'Natesan and Co.'

Hinduism means the 'ism' of the Hindu; and as the word Hindu has been derived from the word Sindhu, the Indus, meaning primarily all the people who reside in the land that extends from Sindhu to Sindhu, Hinduism must necessarily mean the religion or the religions that are peculiar and native to this land and these people. If we are unable to reduce the different tenets and beliefs to a single system of religion then the only way would be to cease to maintain that Hinduism is a system and to say that it is a set of systems consistent with, or if you like, contradictory or even conflicting with, each other. But in no case can you advance this your failure to determine the meaning of Hinduism as a ground to doubt the existence of the Hindu nation itself, or worse still to commit a sacrilege in hurting the feelings of our Avaidik brethren and Vaidik Hindu brethren alike, by relegating any of them to the Non-Hindu pale.

The limits of this essay do not permit us to determine the nature or the essentials of Hinduism or to try to discuss it at any great length. As we have shown above the enquiry into what is Hinduism can only begin after the question 'who is a Hindu?' is rightly answered determining the essentials of Hindutva ; and as it is only with these essentials of Hindutva, which enable us to know who is a Hindu, that this our present enquiry is concerned, the discussion of Hinduism falls necessarily outside of our scope. We have to take cognizance of it only so far as it trespasses on the field of our special charge. Hinduism is a word that properly speaking should be applied to all the religious beliefs that the different communities of the Hindu people hold. But it is generally applied to that system of religion which the majority of the Hindu people follow. It is natural that a religion or a country or community should derive its name from the characteristic feature which is common to an overwhelming majority that constitutes or contributes to it. It is also convenient for easy reference or parlance. But a convenient term that is not only delusive but harmful and positively misleading should not any longer be allowed to blind our judgement. The majority of the Hindus subscribes to that system of religion which could fitly be described by the attribute that constitutes its special feature, as told by *Shruti*. *Smriti* and *Puranas* or *Sanatan Dharma*. They would not object if it even be called *Vaidik Dharma*. But besides these there are other Hindus who reject either partly or wholly, the authority—some of the *Puranas*, some of the Smritis and some of the *Shrutis* themselves. But if you identify the religion of the Hindus with the religion of the majority only and call it orthodox Hinduism, then the different heterodox communities being Hindus themselves rightly resent this usurpation of Hindutva by the majority as well as their unjustifiable exclusion. The religion of the minorities also requires a name. But if you call the so-called orthodox religion alone as Hinduism then naturally it follows that the religion of the so-called heterodox is not Hinduism. The next most fatal step being that, therefore, those sections are not Hindus at all!! But this inference seems as staggering even to those who had unwillingly given whole-hearted support to the premises which have made it logically inevitable that while hating to own it they hardly know to avoid arriving at it. And thus we find that while millions of our Sikhs, Jains, Lingayats, several Samajis and others would deeply resent to be told that they—whose fathers' fathers up to the tenth generation had the blood of Hindus in their veins—had suddenly ceased to be Hindu!—yet a section amongst them takes it most emphatically for granted that they had been faced with a choice that either they should consent to be a party to those customs and beliefs which they had in their puritanic or progressive zeal rejected as superstitions, or they should cease to belong to that race to which their forefathers belonged.

All this bitterness is mostly due to the wrong use of the word, Hinduism, to denote the religion of the majority only. Either the word should be restored to its proper significance to denote the religions of all Hindus or if you fail to do that it should be dropped altogether. The religion of the majority of the Hindus could be best denoted by the ancient accepted appellation, the Sanatan dharma or the Shruti-Smriti-Puranokta Dharma or the Vaidik Dharma; while the religion of the remaining Hindus would continue to be denoted by their respective and accepted names Sikha Dharma or Arya Dharma or Jain Dharma or Buddha Dharma. Whenever the necessity of denoting these Dharmas as a whole arises then alone we may be justified in denoting them by the generic term Hindu Dharma or Hinduism. Thus there would be no loss either in clearness, or in conciseness but on the other hand a gain both in precision and unambiguity which by removing the cause of suspicion in our minor communities and resentment in the major one would once more unite us all Hindus under our ancient banner representing a common race and a common civilization.

The earliest records that we have got of the religious beliefs of any Indian community—not to speak of mankind itself—are the Vedas. The Vedic nation of the Saptasindhus was sub-divided into many a tribes and classes. But although the majority then held a faith that we for simplicity call Vedic religion, yet it was not contributed to by an important minority of the Sindhus themselves. The Panees, the Dasas, the Vratyas and many others from time to time seem to have either seceded from or never belonged to the orthodox church and yet racially and nationally they were conscious of being a people by themselves. There was such a thing as Vedic religion, but it could not even be idenitfied with Sindhu Dharma; for the latter term, had it been coined, would have naturally meant the set of religions prevailing in Saptasindhu, orthodox as well as heterodox. By a process of elimination and assimilation the race of the Sindhus at last grew into the race of Hindus, and the land of the Sindhus, i.e. Sindhustan, into the land of the Hindus, i.e. Hindusthan. While their orthodox and the heterodox schools of religions have,—having tested much, dared much and known much,—having subjected to the most searching examination possible till then, all that lay between the grandest and the tiniest, from the atom to the *Atman*—from the *Paramanu* to the *Parabrahma*,—having sounded the deepest secrets of thoughts and having soared to the highest altitudes of ecstasy,— given birth to a synthesis that sympathises with all aspirants towards truth from the monist to the atheist. Truth was its goal, realization its method. It is neither Vedic nor non-Vedic, it is both. It is the veritable science of religion applied. This is Hindudharma—the conclusion of the conclusions arrived at by harmonising the detailed experience of all the schools of religious thought—Vaidik, Sanatani, Jain, Baudda, Sikha or Devasamaji. Each one and everyone of those systems or sects which are the direct descendants and developments of the religious beliefs Vaidik and non-Vaidik that obtained in the land of the Saptasindhus or in the other unrecorded communities in other parts of India in the Vedic period, belongs to and is an integral part of Hindu Dharma.

Therefore, the Vaidik or the Sanatan Dharma itself is merely a sect of Hinduism or Hindu Dharma, however, overwhelming be the majority that contributes to its tenets. It was a definition of this Sanatan Dharma which the late Lokamanya Tilak framed in the famous verse.

Belief in the Vedas, many means, no strict rule for worship—these are the features of the Hindu religion.

In a learned article that he had contributed to the Chitramayajagat which bears the mark of his deep erudition and insight Lokmanya in an attempt to develop this more or less negative definition into a positive one, had clearly suggested that he had an eye not on Hindutva as such but only on what was popularly called Hindu Dharma, and had also admitted that it could hardly include in its sweep the Aryasamajis and other sects which nevertheless are racially and nationally Hindus of Hindus. That definition, excellent so far as it goes, is in fact not a definition of Hindu Dharma, much less of Hindutva but of Sanatan Dharma—the Shruti-Smriti-Puranokta sect, which being the most popular of all sects of Hindu Dharma was naturally but loosely mistaken for Hindu Dharma itself.

Thus Hindu Dharma being etymologically as well as actually and in its religious aspects only, (for Dharma is not merely religion) the religion of the Hindus, it necessarily partakes of all the essentials that characterise a Hindu. We have found that the first important essential qualification of a Hindu is that to him the land that extends from Sindhu to Sindhu is the Fatherland (*Pitribhu*), the Motherland (*Matribhu*) the land of his patriarchs and forefathers. The system or set of religions which we call Hindu Dharma—Vaidik and Non-Vaidik—is as truly the offspring of this soil as the men whose thoughts they are or who 'saw' the Truth revealed in them. To Hindu Dharma with all its sects and systems this land, Sindhusthan, is the land of its revelation, the land of its birth on this human plane. As the Ganges, though flowing from the lotus feet of Vishnu himself, is even to the most orthodox devotee and mystic so far as human plane is concerned the daughter of the Himalayas, even so, this land is the birth-place—the *Matribhu* (motherland) and the *Pitribhu* (fatherland)—of that Tatvajnana (philosophy) which in its religious aspect is signified as Hindu Dharma. The second most important essential of Hindutva is that a Hindu is a descendant of Hindu parents, claims to have the blood of the ancient Sindhu and the race that sprang from them in his veins. This also is true of the different schools of religion of the Hindus; for they too being either founded by or revealed to the Hindu sages, and seers are the moral and cultural and spiritual descendants and development of the Thought of Saptasindhus through the process of assimilation and elimination, as we are of their seed. Not only is Hindu Dharma the growth of the natural environments and of the thought of the Indus, but also of the *Sanskriti* or culture of the Hindus. The environmental frames in which its scenes, whether of the Vaidik period or of Baudha, Jain or any extremely modern ones of Chaitanya, Chakradhar, Basava, Nanak, Dayananda or Raja Rammohan, are set, the technical terms and the language that furnished expression to its highest revelation and ecstasies, its mythology and its philosophy, the conceptions it controverted and the conceptions it adopted, have the indelible stamp of Hindu culture, of Hindu *Sanskriti*, impressed upon them. Hindu Dharma of all shades and schools, lives and grows and has its being in the atmosphere of Hindu culture, and the Dharma of a Hindu being so completely identified with the land of the Hindus, this land to him is not only a *Pitribhu* but a *Punyabhu*, not only a fatherland but a holyland.

Yes, this Bharatbhumi, this Sindusthan, this land of ours that stretches from Sindhu to Sindhu is our Punyabhumi, for it was in this land that the Founders of our faith and the Seers to whom 'Veda' the Knowledge was revealed, from Vaidik seers to Dayananda, from Jina to Mahavir, from Buddha to Nagasen, from Nanak to Govind, from Banda to Basava, from Chakradhar to Chaitanya, from Ramdas to Rammohan, our *Gurus* and Godmen were born and bred. The very dust of its paths echoes the footfalls of our Prophets and Gurus. Sacred are its rivers, hallowed its groves, for it was either on their moonlit *ghats* or under their eventide long shadows, that the deepest problems of life, of man, soul and God, of Brahma and Maya, were debated and discussed by a Buddha or a Shankar. Ah! every hill and dell is instinct with memories of a Kapil or a Vyas, Shankar or Ramdas. Here Bhagirath rules, there Kurukshetra lies. Here Ramchandra made his first halt of an exile, there Janaki saw the golden deer and fondly pressed her lover to kill it. Here the divine Cowherd played on his flute that made every heart in Gokul dance in harmony as if in a hypnotized sleep. Here is Bodhi Vriksha, here the deer-park, here Mahaveer entered Nirvana. Here stood crowds of worshippers amongst whom Nanak sat and sang the Arati 'the sun and the moon are the lights in the plate of the sky!' Here Gopichand the king look on vows of Gopichand the Jogi and with a bowl in his hand knocked at his sister's door for a handful of alms! Here the son of Bandabahadur was hacked to pieces before the eyes of his father and the young bleeding heart of the son thrust in the father's mouth for the fault of dying as a Hindu! Every stone here has a story of martyrdom to tell! Every inch of thy soil, O Mother! has been a sacrificial ground! Not only 'where the Krishnasar is found' but from Kasmir to Sinhar it is 'Land of sacrifice', sanctified with a *Jnana Yajna* or an *Atmaajna* (self-sacrifice). So to every Hindu, from the Santal to the Sadhu this Bharata *bhumi* this Sindhusthan is at once a *Pitribhu* and a *Punyabhu*—fatherland and a holy land.

That is why in the case of some of our Mohammedan or Christian countrymen who had originally been forcibly converted to a non-Hindu religion and who consequently have inherited along with Hindus, a common Fatherland and a greater part of the wealth of a common culture—language, law, customs, folklore and history—are not and cannot be recognized as Hindus. For though Hindusthan to them is Fatherland as to any other Hindu yet it is not to them a Holyland too. Their holyland is far off in Arabia or Palestine. Their mythology and Godmen, ideas and heroes are not the children of this soil. Consequently, their names and their outlook smack of a foreign origin. Their love is divided. Nay, if some of them be really believing what they profess to do, then there can be no choice—they must, to a man, set their Holy-land above their Fatherland in their love and allegiance. That is but natural. We are not condemning nor are we lamenting.

We are simply telling facts as they stand. We have tried to determine the essentials of Hindutva and in doing so we have discovered that the Bohras and such other Mohammedan or Christian communities possess all the essential qualifications of Hindutva but one and that is that they do not look upon India as their Holyland.

It is not a question of embracing any doctrine propounding any new theory of the interpretation of God, Soul and Man, for we honestly believe that the Hindu Thought—we are not speaking of any religion which is dogma—has exhausted the very possibilities of human speculation as to the nature of the Unknown—if not the Unknowable, or the nature of the relation between that and thou. Are you a monist—a monotheist—a pantheist—an atheist—an agnostic? Here is ample room, O soul ! whatever thou art, to love and grow to thy fullest height and satisfaction in this Temple of temples, that stands on no personal foundation but on the broad and deep and strong foundation of Truth. Why goest then to fill thy little pitcher to wells far off, when thou standest on the banks of the crystal-streamed Ganges herself? Does not the blood in your veins, O brother, of our common forefathers cry aloud with the recollections of the dear old scenes and ties from which they were so cruelly snatched away at the point of the sword? Then come ye back to the fold of your brothers and sisters who with arms extended are standing at the open gate to welcome you—their long lost kith and kin. Where can you find more freedom of worship than in this land where a Charvak could preach atheism from the steps of the temple of Mahakal—more freedom of social organisation than in the Hindu society where from the Patnas of Orissa to the *Pandits* of Benares, from the Santals to the Sadhus, each can develop a distinct social type of polity or organize a new one ? Verily whatever, could be found in the world is found here too. And if anything is not found here it could be found nowhere.

Ye, who by race, by blood, by culture, by nationality possess almost all the essentials of Hindutva and had been forcibly snatched out of our ancestral home by the hand of violence—ye, have only to render wholehearted love to our common Mother and recognize her not only as Fatherland (*Pitribhu*) but even as a Holyland (*Punyabhu*); and ye would be most welcome to the Hindu fold.

This is a choice which our countrymen and our old kith and kin, the Bohras, Khojas, Memons and other Mohammedan and Christian communities are free to make—a choice again which must be a choice of love. But as long as they are not minded thus, so long they cannot be recognized as Hindus. We are, it must be remembered, trying to analyse and determine the essentials of Hindutva as that word is actually understood to signify and would not be justified in straining it in its application to suit any pre-conceived notions or party convenience.

A Hindu, therefore, to sum up the conclusions arrived at, is he who looks upon the land that extends from Sindu to Sindu—from the Indus to the Seas,—as the land of his forefathers—his Fatherland (*Pitribhu*), who inherits the blood of that race whose first discernible source could be traced to the Vedic Saptasindhus and which on its onward march, assimilating much that was incorporated and ennobling much that was assimilated, has come to be known as the Hindu people, who has inherited and claims as his own the culture of that race as expressed chiefly in their common classical language Sanskrit and represented by a common history, a common literature, art and architecture, law and jurisprudence, rites and rituals, ceremonies and sacraments, fairs and festivals; and who above all, addresses this land, this Sindhusthan as his Holyland (*Punyabhu*), as the land of his prophets and seers, of his godmen and *gurus*, the land of piety and pilgrimage. These are the essentials of Hindutva a common nation (*Rashtra*), a common race (*Jati*) and a common civilization (*Sanskriti*). All these essentials could best be summed up by stating in brief that he is a Hindu to whom Sindhusthan is not only a *Pitribhu* but also a *Punyabhu*. For the first two essentials of Hindutva—nation and *Jati*—are clearly denoted and connoted by the word *Pitrubhu* while the third essential of *Sanskriti* is. pre-eminently implied by the word Punyabhu, as it is precisely Sanskriti including *sanskaras*, i.e. rites and rituals, ceremonies and sacraments, that makes a land a Holyland. To make the definition more handy, we may be allowed to compress it in a couplet:

—A Sindu Sindhu paryanta, Yasya Bharatbhumika Pitribhuh
Punyabhushchaiva sa vai Hinduriti smritah

[*Source*: Savarkar, V.D. (1969). *Hindutva*. Mumbai: Veer Savarkar Prakashan]

Bibliography

Ambedkar, B.R. (1936). *Annihilation of Caste.* Bombay: New Books Co.

Ambedkar, B.R.(1955). *Thoughts of Linguistic States.* Aurangabad: Milind Mahavidyalaya.

Babasaheb Ambedkar: Writings and Speeches (*BAWS*), Vol. 1, 3, 4, . New Delhi: Dr. Ambedkar Foundation, Ministry of Social Justice & Empowerment, Government of India.

Chitragupta. (1987). *Life of Barrister Savarkar*. Bombay: Veer Savarkar Prakashan. https://savarkar.org/en/pdfs/life_of_barrister_savarkar_by_chitragupta.pdf.

Keer, Dhananjay (2013). *Dr. Babasaheb Ambedkar*. Bombay: Popular Prakashan.

Keer, Dhananjay. (1950). *Savarkar and His Times*. Bombay: A.V. Keer.

Ambedkar. B. R. (2017). *Ambedkar: The Attendant Details*, Yusufji, Salim (ed.), New Delhi: Navayana.

Gandhi, M.K. (1922).*Speeches and Writings of Mahatma Gandhi*. Madras: G.K Nasan and Co.

Gandhi. M.K. (1954).*The Removal of Untouchability* (ed.) B. Kumarrapa. Ahmedabad: Navajivan.

Gandhi, M.K. (1955). *My Religion*. Ahmedabad: Navajivan.

Gandhi, M.K. (1996). *The Essence of Hinduism*. Ahmedabad: Navajivan.

Gandhi, M.K. (1994). *What is Hinduism?* New Delhi: National Book Trust.

Gandhi. M.K. (2015). *An Autobiography or The Story of My Experiments with Truth*. Ahmedabad: Navajivan.

Julia Kelley-Swift. (2015). *A Misunderstood Legacy: V.D. Savarkar and the Creation of Hindutva.* A thesis submittedto the faculty of Wesleyan University. Middletown, Connecticut.http://citeseerx.ist.psu.edu/viewdoc/download pdf. Downloaded on 26 June 2020.

Jyotirmaya Sharma. (2007). "History as Revenge and Retaliation: Rereading Savarkar's 'the War of Independence of 1857'," *Economic and Political Weekly,* 42, No. 19: 1718.

Pantham, T. (2009). 'Against Untouchability: The Discourse of Gandhi and Ambedkar' in Gopal Guru (ed.) *Humiliation.* New Delhi: Oxford University Press.

Parekh, Bhikhu. (1991). *Gandhi's Political Philosophy: A Critical Examination*. London: Palgrave Macmillan.

Prabhhu, R.K. and U.R. Rao. (2008). *The Mind of Mahatma* . Ahmedabad: Navajivan.

Paul Schaffel. (2012). "Empire and Assassination: Indian Students, 'India House', and Information Gathering in Great Britain, 1898-1911" (Wesleyan University, 2012) http://www.pwsfoundation.org/pdfs/PWS_Schaffel_Paul_2012_Thesis.pdf .

Savarkar, V.D. (1969). *Hindutva*. Bombay: Veer Savarkar Prakashan.

Savarkar, V.D. *Hindu Rashtra Darshan* (HRD) https://fdocuments.in/download/hindu-rashtra-darshan-v-d-savarkarpdf.html

Sampath, Vikram. (2019). *Savarkar Echoes from a Forgotten Past 1883-1924*, India: Penguin.

The Collected Works of Mahatma Gandhi, Vols.1-100 (*CWMG*-KS-1956-1994). New Delhi: Publication Division, The Government of India. Retrieved from https://www.gandhiheritageportal.org/. CWMG Vols.1-100.

Index